AMAZING FLOPS AND FIASCOS

BRENDA APSLEY
ILLUSTRATED BY KIM BLUNDELL

OCTOPUS BOOKS

First published in 1988 by
Octopus Books Limited
Michelin House
81 Fulham Road
London, SW3 6RB

Cover by Mik Brown

ISBN 0 7064 3291 6

Printed in the United Kingdom

Introduction

Have you heard about the cold cure that left patients with cold toes, the bats that burned down an American air base, or Jack Mytton's drastic cure for his hiccups? Do you know about the man who said that machines heavier than air would never fly, the farmers who painted their milk cows in bright colours and patterns to stop keen deer hunters shooting them by mistake, or the film that lost $57,000,000 and closed a Hollywood studio?

They all have something in common – they are ideas that failed badly, schemes that flopped miserably. In this book, you can read about more than 150 of the world's funniest, silliest, wackiest, almost unbelievable flops and failures. And they all have something else in common – believe it or not, they really happened!

Canute Can't . . .

Canute II was the Danish King of England who ruled the country from about 955 to 1035 AD. His followers wanted to show how all-powerful he was, and devised a test. The King sat on a beach at the water's edge and ordered the waves to go back. The waves still rolled in, and the test was abandoned as a failure when the King's feet got wet . . .

I Do, I Do, I Do, I Do, I Do

Mrs Beverley Avery of Los Angeles, California, USA, is a real failure in the marriage stakes. By 1957, she had been divorced 16 times, from 14 husbands (twice from two of them). She said that five of her husbands had broken her nose . . .

Good News is No News

Good News was a newspaper launched in Sacramento, California, USA, in 1970. It was a newspaper with a difference – as its name suggests, it printed only good news. Robberies, crimes, deaths and disasters did not feature on its pages. That was the good news. The bad news was that it didn't sell very well, and it soon folded and failed. Its last edition carried headlines like '196,458,483 citizens were not killed in auto accidents this year', and, 'No wars declared in sixteen weeks'.

Situation Vacant

The Jobcentre at Grantham in eastern England had 600 unemployed women on its books who were looking for work, but the Jobcentre still couldn't fill a vacancy that paid £10 per night (good rates in 1982). The manager

of the centre failed to find one woman who would even consider the job. Maybe it was because the vacancy was offered by Buffalo Billy Wild, a knife-thrower. He wanted to employ a new human target to throw knives at!

Blue Peter

Peter Duncan, a presenter on *Blue Peter* (a British children's television programme) decided to cross the Irish Sea from Scotland to Northern Ireland. What was so unusual about that? Well, Peter planned to make the 40 kilometre (25 mile) crossing between Portpatrick and Bangor not in a boat, but in a small Volkswagen Beetle car fitted with a propellor and buoyancy aids. Peter set off on 9 March, 1985, but didn't get far. In spite of running repairs to the generator at sea, the Beetle had to be towed home by the escort boat, and Peter's nautical 'drive' was a soggy failure.

They Saw Through Shearer

During World War One, English soldier Sergeant James Shearer, who served as an auxiliary nurse, claimed that he had developed a new and superior version of the x-ray machine. X-rays had only been discovered a few years earlier, and the machines had aroused a lot of scientific interest. Doctors asked Shearer to demonstrate his machine, which he called a delineator.

The box-shaped machine was set up at the battlefront in France, and a wounded soldier stood in front of it. The delineator whirred and whizzed for a few moments, then a piece of paper emerged from its side, with the man's internal organs clearly marked on it. Army doctors were impressed – and they became very interested when Shearer claimed that the delineator could detect enemy aircraft, too, if pointed skywards.

But how did the machine work? Officers ordered Shearer to open the box. Inside they found just the working parts of a pianola, a mechanical piano operated by air pressure. The x-ray machine and enemy aircraft spotter failed on the spot – and so did Sergeant Shearer's career.

Crash

Frenchman Albert Sauvent announced that he had developed a new plane – a crash-proof design that could withstand any accident. He would not reveal how he had made the plane crash-proof, but agreed to test it himself. In 1932, Monsieur Sauvent had the plane carried to the top of a high cliff near Nice, in the south of France. He then sat in the plane, and it was pushed off the edge of the cliff, crashing to the ground thousands of metres below. Amazingly, Monsieur Sauvent walked away from the crash with just a few bruises, but the plane was wrecked. The crash-proof plane had proved itself a flying flop . . .

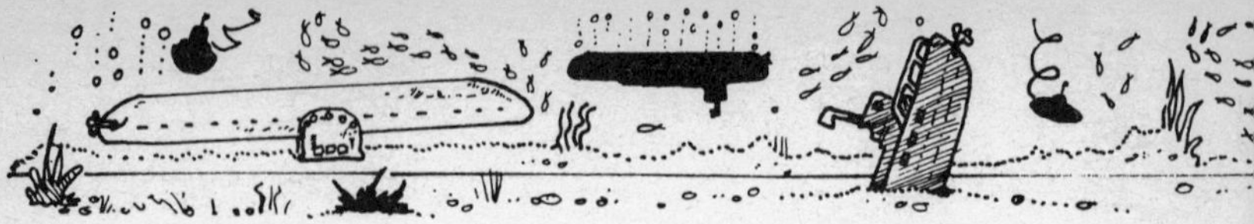

Ve Haf Vays of Making You Talk!

The biggest flop as a phrase book has to be the one issued to German soldiers during World War Two. The book gave the soldiers lots of useful phrases to memorize, should they find themselves in enemy territory in Britain. The phrases included: 'Open all cupboards', 'Give me opium', 'I have a stomach ache', and, 'You will wash two shirts, one pair of trousers and three handkerchiefs'. A spy could go far with conversation like that . . .

First Night, Last Night

Alan Jay Lerner was a very successful American lyricist and writer who worked on hit musicals *Camelot, Gigi* and *My Fair Lady,* so when his new show *Dance a Little Closer* opened on Broadway, the critics all attended the first night. Alas, they hated the show, and that first night was also the show's last night.

Butler 1, Mistress 0

The most awful failure at controlling her servants has to be society hostess Mrs Warner. At her home in London, England, she was giving a very grand dinner party one evening, and was anxious that everything went well.

Her butler had other ideas. He was very drunk, and behaved badly throughout the meal. Mrs Warner gave him meaningful looks, and whispered orders that he should behave, but the butler took no notice, and staggered around the room. Mrs Warner was furious when the butler spilled sauce down the front of her dress, and scribbled a note which she handed to him. 'You are drunk,' the note said, 'leave the room at once.'

The butler glanced quickly at the note, then put it on his tray and walked to the far end of the table, where he handed it to the guest of honour, the famous statesman, Sir Winston Churchill. What Sir Winston thought of being ordered from the room by Mrs Warner, we do not know! What we *do* know is that in that particular master-versus-servant battle, the butler was the definite winner!

Wrong, Dear Doctor

Doctor Dionysius Lardner was a well-respected professor of astronomy at University College in London, England. He stated that if trains reached speeds of 120 kilometres per hour (75 miles per hour) passengers would be unable to breathe, and would die. Wrong. Passengers can travel by train at speeds of 500 kilometres per hour (310 miles per hour) with no ill effects.

Doctor Lardner also stated that no large steamship would ever be able to cross the Atlantic Ocean because it would need more coal for fuel than it could carry. His theory failed just a few years later when, in 1838, the steamship, *Great Western*, made the first crossing.

Rock On, Abraham

Thousands of people gathered in the shopping precinct in Northgate, Seattle, USA, to watch the unveiling of a new statue by the sculptor Rieske, in 1973. A hushed silence fell as the drapes were pulled free to reveal a huge, 4.8 metre (16 foot) statue of Abraham Lincoln, the 16th president of the United States. And this was no ordinary statue . . .

The sculptor pressed a hidden button and the statue's arms and lips began to move, then a tapedeck hidden in the moving head started up, and the beginning of one of the President's famous speeches boomed across the precinct through speakers in his hands. The crowd was amazed, and the sculptor congratulated himself on his success.

The success was short-lived, though. A powerful signal from a local rock radio station swamped the circuits in the statue, and instead of Lincoln's dignified words, a loud rock song began to boom across the square. The statue, head and arms still moving, danced along . . .

Gulp!

In the 1920s, a young American had what he thought was a great money-making idea. No one liked taking medicine because it tasted so awful, so what if he came up with a medicine shield that fitted over the tongue, so masking the taste? Surely he would sell thousands? Wrong! The idea flopped badly because, with the device fitted over the tongue, the patient couldn't swallow! It didn't help the medicine go down at all.

Vampire Repellent

Ian Dbworski was a Polish emigrant who made his home in Stoke-on-Trent, northern England. Jan lived in fear of attacks by vampires (though there had never been a vampire sighting in Stoke) and was convinced that the nasty blood-suckers would get him if he didn't ward them off. Every night Jan went to bed with garlic cloves tied around his neck, and with a clove in his mouth. He believed the garlic would keep him safe.

Sadly, it didn't, and Jan was found dead in 1966. Had the vampires struck after all? No – Jan had choked on the clove of garlic in his mouth. As a vampire repellent, the garlic was a success, but as a late-night snack it was a fatal failure.

The Fifty Million Dollar Flying Flop

Howard Hughes was an eccentric American millionaire who liked developing new planes. He spent $50,000,000 on a plane that could take off and land on water, and called the flying boat *Hercules*. It was a vast plane with eight engines, designed to carry 750 passengers or 362,880 kilograms (800,150 pounds) of cargo. Because of a shortage of raw materials, the plane was built in wood, and because of this it was nicknamed the Spruce Goose. When the flying boat was ready for trials, Hughes decided to conduct these himself. On 2 November, 1947, he flew the craft to an altitude of 21 metres (60 feet), for a distance of just 1.6 kilometres (1 mile), then said he wasn't impressed, and labelled the project a complete and utter failure. He cancelled all work on the huge and costly plane there and then, and it was never resumed.

Bath-Time Blues

John Roy of Weeley, Essex, in south-east England, has an unusual hobby – moustache-growing. He grew his whiskers to a record-breaking 189 centimetres (74½ inches), but in 1984 fame turned to flop when Mr Roy took a bath. He sat on his moustache, accidentally chopped 61 centimetres (24 inches) from one side, and lost his record.

A Fishy Story

Thomas Birch was an 18th-century English scholar. He was a very keen, but not very successful, fisherman, and he tried all sorts of ideas to improve his angling – new rods, different baits, unusual flies. Nothing seemed to work. Then one day Thomas had what he thought was a brilliant realization – the fish must be able to see him on the bank and be frightened

off. The solution he came up with was equally brilliant – he would disguise himself so that he could get close to the fish, and catch them off-guard.

Thomas put his plan into action. He built a large disguise that made him look like a tree, with his body in the trunk, two holes for his eyes, and his arms in outstretched branches. He even stuck leaves on to the branches to make the tree look more life-like. Thomas stood by the river bank all day long, but his idea was a dismal failure. He still didn't catch any fish, and his idea didn't catch on . . .

Plop!

Andy Aish, of Taunton, in south-west England, set out to cross the River Avon on 22 August, 1985. Over a bridge, in a boat, swimming? No – Andy planned to jump the river in his car. The jump failed miserably, and Andy ended up in the water. Maybe the jump failed because he was towing a caravan behind his car at the time . . .

A Model Failure

When the British Broadcasting Corporation built new headquarters beside their old base in London, England, and connected the two buildings with narrow corridors, the music department realized they had a problem. How would they be able to move their large grand pianos from room to room? The music department didn't want to risk damaging their valuable pianos on a trial run, so BBC carpenters came up with what seemed like a good idea. They would build a full-size wooden model grand piano that the music people could try moving along the narrow corridors, without any risk to the real pianos. The model was built, but the plan failed miserably when the carpenters tried to deliver it, and found that it was too big to go through the workshop doors . . .

Clippety Flop

The Greek shipping millionaire Stavros Niarchos is good at making money, but a bit of a flop at spotting a winner. At the 1985 Newmarket sales in England, he bought a racehorse called Fusion. At £600,000 it was the most

expensive yearling in Europe. Fusion was put into training, but after two years he had won only two fourth places. As a racehorse he was, frankly, a failure.

Mr Niarchos admitted defeat, and in 1987 sold the horse to an Irish trainer, Tommy Wade. Fusion's price? Just £15,000.

Hic!

Most people have their own favourite cure for hiccups – blowing into a paper bag, drinking from the wrong side of a cup, or even pinching the end of their nose. A man called Jack Mytton had tried all the usual cures, but they had failed to stop his hiccups, so he decided to try out an idea of his own. It was rather drastic, and designed to shock him into forgetting his hiccups. Jack's idea didn't catch on with other sufferers though – it entailed setting fire to his nightshirt while he was still wearing it!

To The Rescue!

The biggest flop as a samaritan is probably Geoffrey Oliver of Falmouth, in south-west England. One day, he looked out of his house and saw a car parked in the road with its engine running. Inside the car he saw a man slumped forward over the steering wheel. Fearing that the man was trying to commit suicide by breathing in poisonous fumes from the car's exhaust system, Mr Oliver ran out to save him. He smashed the car's front window, wrenched open the door, and dragged the man into the road.

Mr Oliver was about to start mouth-to-mouth resuscitation when the 'suicide' sat up and started shouting at him. He told Mr Oliver that he hadn't been trying to kill himself – he'd simply decided to take a nap in his car, and had left the engine running to keep warm. As a would-be rescuer, Mr Oliver had failed miserably.

Bland Bungles Blackmail

Blackmailer William Bland of Pennsylvania, USA, demanded over $500,000 from a rich factory owner. If he refused to pay up, Bland threatened to reveal some secrets that

the man would prefer not to be known. The factory owner agreed to pay, and arrangements were made for the hand-over of the money. 'How do you want the money?' asked the factory owner. 'In used bank notes?'

Bland, who wasn't a very experienced blackmailer, thought for a moment, then told the man that he wanted the money paid into his bank account. And that's where the plan failed. Bland gave the factory owner his name and his bank account number, and the man gave it to the police. Bland was arrested soon after.

Goose Bumps

A beach was opened just outside the city of Newcastle-upon-Tyne, in north-east England, in the summer of 1987. This was not just any ordinary beach – it was for the use of nudists only, and City councillors thought it would attract lots of visitors to the area. Alas, they had forgotten that the British climate can be very unkind. Skies were grey, rain fell, and temperatures plummeted. Months later, not one visitor had been to the beach.

Arbroath 36, Bon Accord 0

The biggest set of combined failures has to be the members of the Bon Accord soccer team, who played in a Scottish Cup match against Arbroath on 12 September, 1885. Arbroath scored no less than 36 goals, with another seven disallowed for offside. Bon Accord? They didn't score once.

The soccer match that failed to pull in the crowds has to be the match played between English Football League teams, Stockport County and Leicester City on 7 May, 1921. In a stadium that held thousands, just 13 fans turned up to watch the match.

The Not-So-Great Griffith

In Frostburg, Maryland, USA, a hypnotist called The Great Griffith arrived in town one day. He claimed to be the best hypnotist in the business, and to prove it, he said he could put anyone in the town to sleep for six days and nights. He asked for a volunteer, but no one stepped forward. Then a young boy raised his hand. 'I'm visting my aunt here in Frostburg,' said the boy. 'She'll be glad to be rid of me for six days. I volunteer.'

The Great Griffith hypnotized the boy, who fell into a deep sleep at once. He was laid in a shop window so that all the townspeople could see him, fast asleep. There he stayed for two days and nights, still and quiet. The people of Frostburg were impressed.

One person was doubtful, though, and that night Harry Reichenbach crept close to the hypnotized boy. 'Psst,' he whispered, 'The Great Griffith sent me. Are you all right?' 'Tell him I'm OK,' replied the 'sleeping' boy, and The Great Griffith's fake failed on the spot.

Never Work With Animals

Richard Whiteley is a well-known quiz show host and reporter on British television. He's best remembered for an interview that turned from fact-finding to fiasco in just a few seconds. Richard had just started interviewing a man about his ferret, when the ferret bit his finger – hard. The ferret wouldn't release its grip, and Richard spent the rest of the interview hopping around the studio in agony with a ferret hanging from his finger!

The Fraud That Flopped

Peter Barrington-Smythe was a con-man who lived in Britain in the 1930s. He thought he had the perfect fraud. Each morning he bought a copy of *The Times* newspaper, not for the news, but for the death notices. He wrote out an invoice and sent it to each of the people who had died, claiming payment for a non-existent umbrella. And not just any old umbrella – one with a very expensive silver handle. The relatives always paid the bills promptly, and Barrington-Smythe made a good living. His fraud flopped, however, when he sent out his usual invoice to an old lady who had died. Her relatives became suspicious right away, for the old lady had spent the past 20 years in bed. Why on earth would she have ordered an umbrella? The police were called, Barrington-Smythe was arrested, and his 'foolproof' fraud had failed . . .

Pot Black . . and Blue

An Australian snooker player wanted his name to go down in the history of the game. He wanted to get into the snooker record books by coming up with a new trick shot – one that no one else had attempted. After a lot of

thought and planning, he announced that he was ready to show off his new shot, and a large crowd gathered to watch.

The player tied balloons filled with helium (so that they floated) to his wrists, and had his legs tied to the roof rafters. He was about to try the world's first suspended snooker shot. Sadly, the shot was a fatal failure – the player fell head first on to the table, cracked his skull, and died.

Turn Off

T*urn On* was a new comedy series that was broadcast on the American ABC television network. Its producers said the show would run and run. Their prediction was very wrong. *Turn On* went out for the first time in 1969 – and was cancelled after the first show.

Anyone for Maggot Burgers?

A daily intake of Vitamin C is important for health. Fresh fruits and vegetables are good sources of Vitamin C – but they are also expensive, so scientists started to look at other, cheaper sources. They came up with a very plentiful, cheap food that is rich in Vitamin C, but soon hit a big problem. How do you persuade people to eat maggots? Tell them, 'a maggot a day keeps the doctor away'? Mince the maggots and serve them as maggot burgers? Add macaroni maggots to the menu? The scientists had to admit failure; maggots are never going to top anyone's list of favourite foods.

Death Ray? No Way!

In 1924, a Mr Grindel-Matthews went to the British Air Ministry with a revolutionary idea – a 'death ray' that would prove a valuable weapon in wartime. The Air Ministry officers were invited to a demonstration of its powers in Mr Grindel-Matthews' laboratory. There he lit an electric lamp, and pointed it at a motor cycle engine some 14 metres (46 feet) away. The 'death ray' stopped the engine running immediately. 'Think what it could do to enemy aircraft,' said Mr Grindel-Matthews. 'My death ray would put them out of action.'

The Air Ministry was interested, but wanted to see the death ray in action on a motor engine supplied by the government, rather than the one supplied by the inventor. They offered him £1,000 if the demonstration was successful.

Suddenly, Mr Grindel-Matthews became less confident and refused the offer. As *The Times* newspaper reported on 28 March: 'It is understood that he has left the country.' Taking his death ray with him, presumably . . .

A Tall Story

Glenn Kalina escaped from a jail in California, USA, in 1983. He was soon recaptured and appeared in court, where the judge asked him how he had escaped. Kalina thought for a moment, then replied that he had escaped by accident while practising pole vaulting in the prison yard. The judge looked interested, so Kalina continued. He explained that he had vaulted higher than ever before, and when he landed, had found himself outside the prison walls. The judge asked why he hadn't gone back in. Kalina had an answer. 'I couldn't find the door,' he replied. 'I walked around for a while, then the guards found me.'

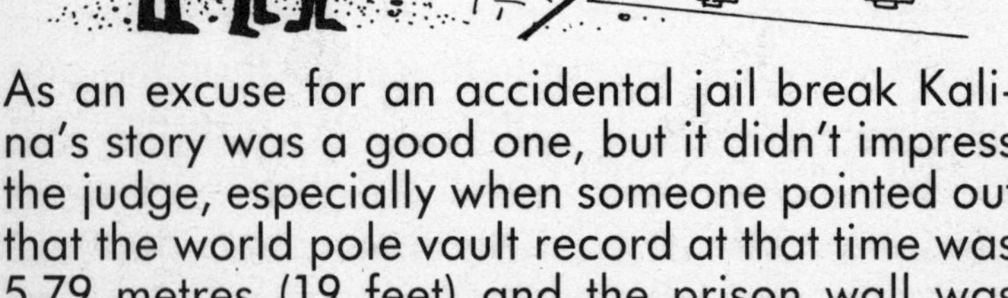

As an excuse for an accidental jail break Kalina's story was a good one, but it didn't impress the judge, especially when someone pointed out that the world pole vault record at that time was 5.79 metres (19 feet) and the prison wall was 6.09 metres (20 feet) high! Kalina's flimsy excuse failed, and he was sentenced to an extra three years in jail.

Souper Idea

Workers at the Campbell's soup factory in Ohio, USA, complained to the management that lifting heavy cases of soup cans caused them back trouble. Managers were sympathetic, and gave the problem a lot of thought. Finally, they came up with a new worker to help out – a robot that cost the company more than $200,000 to develop. The idea was that the robot would lift the cases of soup, rather than the workers.

It sounded good on paper, but when the robot started work, it caused chaos. Whenever the robot found a faulty case, it dropped it, and caused many thousands of dollars-worth of damage. Campbell's had to admit that their robot was a failure; it was fired and sent to a local university. For the workers, it was a case of back to backache . . .

Who Needs an Umbrella?

Frank Galton was a man of ideas – lots of them. One question he thought about was how best to keep clothes dry in the rain. Frank soon came up with what he thought was the perfect solution – when it rained, he simply took off all his clothes, folded them up, and sat on them until the rain stopped. Not surprisingly, the idea failed to catch on!

Concerto for One

A not very well-known composer called Riley wrote a piece he called *Concerto In C*. To the composer's surprise, every member of the audience – and most of the orchestra – left the concert hall before the end of the first performance of the work. Why? Maybe it was something to do with the four-hour piece being played in the dark, and the complete absence of a tune; the *Concerto In C* consisted of the same note being struck over and over again. The piece was labelled a flop, and has never been heard in public since then.

A Jewel of a Story

The customs official on the border between Belgium and Germany thought he had made a great find when he stopped a couple from London, England, in September 1987, and asked them what they had in their baggage. Instead of the usual, 'Clothes and souvenirs,' Susan and and Nicholas Findeisen replied, 'The British Crown Jewels.' The official searched their luggage . . . and found more than 200 jewel-studded crowns, orbs, tiaras and sceptres. Thinking that he had foiled a massive theft, the customs officer held the Findeisens for 12 hours while he checked that the Crown Jewels (worth many millions of pounds) were still in the Tower of London.

What the customs official had failed to understand was that the jewels were exact copies of the original jewels, on their way to an exhibition in Bonn, Germany. And that wasn't the first time the Findeisens and their jewels had failed to clear customs. When they took the display to America, a woman customs officer wouldn't let them pass until she had tried on one of the many glittering crowns . . .

A Slippery Customer

Lots of Spanish houses are fitted with iron grilles over doors and windows so that they can be left open for fresh air whilst remaining secure. One thief, who had used a duplicate key to get into a house, was searching for valuables when he heard the owners returning. He fled into the bedroom and tried to escape through a window, but couldn't quite squeeze through the narrow gaps between the iron bars. Then he had an idea. He took off all his clothes, smeared himself with cold cream, and was able to slip out through the bars. But his plan failed when police arrested him in the street outside. They wanted to know why he was walking around with no clothes on, completely covered in cold cream . . .

All at Sea

In 1875, war raged in Europe, with the French army fighting against the forces of Britain, Austria and Holland (now The Netherlands). During a period of intensely cold weather in January, a French general called Charles Pichegru led his troop of mounted cavalry soldiers towards the Dutch city of Amsterdam.

As the soldiers and their horses travelled across the frozen, snow-covered countryside, they saw the whole of the Dutch fleet lying off the island of Texel. General Pichegru wondered why the ships were there, and not sailing out to sea. As he and his troops drew nearer, General Pichegru found the answer – the Dutch ships were frozen into the sea in heavy ice, and could not move! The General realized that he had the whole Dutch navy just where he wanted them, and ordered his troops to attack. The troops rode their horses across the thick ice, and soon overpowered the stranded sailors, capturing their ships. With their entire navy in enemy hands, the Dutch government had to admit defeat and surrender. Thanks to the weather, the Dutch navy had proved an embarrassing flop as a fighting force . . .

If At First You Don't Succeed . . .

Try, try, try again. That must be the personal motto of Naresh Savita of Kanpur, in eastern India. He has tried to commit suicide no less than 21 times – and failed every attempt. He has taken drug overdoses, and has even tried swallowing a lizard in his repeated efforts to end it all. His latest suicide attempt failed like all the others when he jumped from a window in a tall apartment block. He suffered just a couple of broken bones.

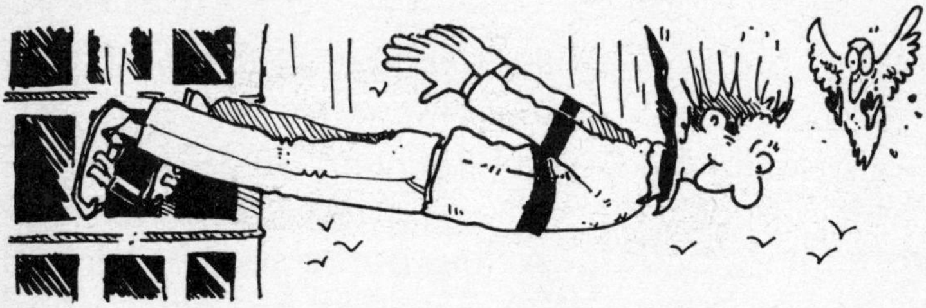

Spots in Front of His Eyes

The Manhattan Center, in New York, USA, was the scene chosen by Bob Specas in June 1978, for a world record-breaking attempt at setting up – and toppling down – thousands of dominoes. Bob spent days setting up rows of dominoes – 97,500 in all. He still had many thousands to position, when disaster struck in the form of a TV cameraman who was cover-

ing the event. He dropped his press badge accidentally, and set off the rows of dominoes before Bob could stop them. The dominoes crashed to the floor, the world record attempt failed, and Bob declared the event a complete fiasco . . .

Fumbling Felons

Thieves held up a store in a suburb of Manchester, northern England, in September 1987. Three men wearing masks and carrying guns burst into the Open Late Saver store and got away with about £3,000 in cash. Police think the gang may have been wearing very thick woolly mittens, as they managed to drop most of the money outside the shop! They panicked, and ran off with just £200!

Robot Power

General Juan Peron, the ruler of Argentina, South America, announced in March 1951 that scientists in his country knew how to harness atomic energy without using uranium. The world sat up and took notice. If this were true, it was a remarkable scientific advance.

General Peron stated that a number of electronic robots were hard at work in the Huemel Island atomic plant, producing atomic energy and doing the work of 500 men. General Peron promised that more details would be released later. They never were, and we have to assume that the far-fetched plan failed miserably.

Excess Baggage

Police guarding the border between France and Spain became suspicious when they saw a small van travelling very slowly towards the frontier post. Though only the driver was in it, the Renault 4 (one of the smallest commercial vehicles in France) looked over-

laden, and leaned backwards so that the back bumper almost touched the ground. Suspecting that the van was being used for smuggling, they checked it over. In the small space at the back of the van they found 16 illegal immigrants! As a way of getting into France secretly, the operation was a failure; as a way of proving that there's more space than you think in the back of a Renault 4, it was a huge success!

Whose Idea Was This, Anyway?

In 1963, the city council of Leeds, in northern England, decided to build a new swimming pool complex. 'As we're going to build a new pool anyway, why don't we make it an international standard pool, and apply to stage the next Commonwealth Games here?' one councillor suggested. Great idea, thought the others, and four years later the expensive new complex was opened.

Unfortunately, the bid by Leeds to host the games failed – someone had taken the wrong measurements, and the swimming pool was a little too small for international competitions. And to add insult to injury, the roof started to collapse, and the pool sprang a leak . . .

Sssssssh!

Ferdinand Waldo Demara Junior was born in Massachusetts, USA, in 1921. He was known as The Great Imposter for his impersonation skills. Early in his 'career', he decided to pretend to be a Trappist monk, and practised how to walk, move . . . and speak. This particular fraud was a real flop – as Ferdinand soon found out, his practise was a waste of time, for Trappist monks take a vow of silence, and don't speak at all!

Call This a Race?

The London to Brighton car run takes place every year when old vintage and veteran cars travel from England's capital, London, to Brighton on the south coast. It's a popular event that attracts thousands of spectators, but the first time the race was held, on 14 November, 1896, the race was a real flop.

54 cars entered the race, but due to engine trouble, only 30 set off. 13 cars broke down en route for Brighton, so that only 17 finished the

race. The Mayor of Brighton and other important guests welcomed the first car to finish – then had to wait another two hours for the second one to cross the line! As a spectator sport the race was about as exciting as snail racing!

Atishoo!

When you gotta sneeze, you gotta sneeze. Janice Ball did, when she drove into a car parking lot in New Jersey, USA. Her failure to stop a sneeze cost her insurance company more than $100,000 in damages paid out to 15 car owners. When Janice sneezed her car shot forward, hit two parked cars, then bounced back to hit another one behind her. This set off a chain reaction as another 12 cars behind her skidded into each other . . . You can bet that sneeze brought tears to Janice's eyes.

Blast Off!

The Russian people are successful in many areas of life, but as television set makers they are real failures. The Russian magazine, *Ogonyuk* reported that in the last five years nearly 1,000 people were killed when their television sets burst into flames! Maybe they should sell them with a handy fire extinguisher attached!

The Parrot Painter

A well-respected abstract artist from Los Angeles, USA, had promised her agent new canvases for a big exhibition they had planned. Some paintings were delivered, but then they suddenly stoped arriving. When asked why, the artist had to explain that she hadn't painted the abstracts – they were the work of her one-eyed parrot, Rajah, who had produced over 1,000 oils and watercolours. But why had Rajah stopped painting? He had been eaten by a cat. As you might have guessed by now, the exhibition was a flop.

Water Power

John Keely was an American man with ideas – very big ideas. One of them was a new and revolutionary power source that he called vibratory energy. He wouldn't give details of how his idea worked, but gave demonstrations in his laboratory that were very impressive. He showed how an egg-cup full of water would fuel a huge engine for weeks, and made a model of an engine that would power a ship across the Atlantic Ocean using no other fuel than .5 litre (1 pint) of water. His demonstrations and models were so good, that, in 1874, he persuaded wealthy backers to give him $1,000,000 to develop his discovery.

John Kelly died in 1898, having spent all the money and returned not one cent to his investors, who searched his laboratory to look for details of his amazing power source. They found something all right – but not what they had hoped for. Kelly's models had been fuelled not by water and vibratory energy, but by compressed air fed to them through thin, hidden tubes. The investors had failed to spot a fraud and a faker.

Head You Win, Tails I Lose

A thief decided to rob a large store in Los Angeles, California, USA. His plan was ultra-simple, and couldn't go wrong – or so he thought. He would take a trolley around the store, collect a few items, then go to a quiet check-out desk. He would watch as the assistant tilled in the goods, then offer her a $100 note as payment. When she opened the cash drawer to get the change, he would simply grab all the money in the drawer, and make his escape.

Things went according to plan. The thief waited as the check-out girl tilled in the goods, then he handed over his $100 bill. As the cash drawer opened, the thief made a grab for the money inside, and ran out of the store. What the thief didn't know was that the till had just been emptied, so he got away with just one ten-dollar bill. And the check-out girl was still holding his $100 bill, so the thief had lost $90 on the deal! 'Have a nice day, sir,' said the manager, cheerfully. 'Call again anytime.' With thieves like that, who needs customers?

The One-Day War

Great Britain and Zanzibar (now part of Tanzania, in eastern Africa) fought a little-known war in 1896. The British battle fleet under Rear Admiral Rawson warned the ruler, Sultan Said Khalid, to leave his palace and surrender his people. When the Sultan refused, Rawson ordered his guns to fire at the palace. The bombardment started on 27 August at 9.02 in the morning – and stopped at 9.40 the same morning when the Sultan surrendered. The world's shortest war was really a bit of a flop, for it had lasted just 38 minutes!

Talent Spotter

This boy can't sing a note,' read the school report from a school in Memphis, Tennessee, USA. 'It would be a good thing if he stopped having music lessons.' As a talent spotter, the teacher who wrote those words proved a real failure – the report was Elvis Presley's – The King of Rock and Roll.

All at Sea

In 1935, the British Broadcasting Corporation sent Commander Woodroffe to commentate on a Royal Naval Review. As darkness fell, the whole fleet was to be lit up, and Woodroffe was to describe the scene live to thousands of radio listeners.

Commander Woodroffe spent the day eating and drinking with old friends, and by the time the lights were switched on he was a little drunk . . .

'The fleet's lit up,' his commentary began. 'When I say lit up, I mean lit up by fairy lights . . . it isn't a fleet at all . . . the whole fleet is in fairyland. We are going to fire a rocket . . . we are going to fire all sorts of things. The whole thing is fairyland . . . it's gone, it's gone . . . it's disappeared. We have two hundred warships all round us . . . now they've all gone. There's nothing between us and heaven . . . there's nothing at all.'

At this point, the listeners were 'returned to the studio'. As a live commentator, the Commander had failed.

Bee Off!

Money production in Brazil, South America, wasn't very successful. The Brazilian bees were lazy, and just weren't working hard enough to produce honey to meet demand. How could Brazil produce more honey? That was the problem put to Doctor Kerr of Sao Paolo University.

Doctor Kerr pondered the problem, then came up with this idea: he would breed a new strain of bee by crossing African queen bees with worker bees from Italy. He believed the new bees would be strong, hard workers that would produce lots of honey.

The bees were strong all right. They were fierce and ferocious and, as Doctor Kerr discovered when thousands escaped, they stung anything that moved. And their sting was deadly. When 150 humans and thousands of animals were stung to death, the new bees were doomed to failure. They were killed, and the relieved Brazilians welcomed back their old lazy bees and their honey with open arms.

McKinney Welcomes Careful Drivers

McKinney, Texas, USA, is usually a pretty quiet town, but that all changed on 15 October, 1966, when a 75 year-old driver took his car out on to the road. In just 20 minutes he had committed four hit-and-run offences, caused six traffic accidents, driven on the wrong side of the road four times, and got ten traffic tickets!

Is That So?

Aristotle, who lived in Greece from 384 to 322 BC, made many important early discoveries, and is thought of as the 'father' of physical and biological science. But some of his ideas failed. He claimed that the heart, and not the brain, was the source of intelligence, and that living creatures could reproduce themselves without 'parents' – that insects, for example, could grow from mud! Which goes to prove that no one is right all the time . . .

The Tapeworm Trap

Doctor Meyers worked in Sheffield, a city in northern England, in the 1870s. Many of his patients suffered from tapeworms – parasitic worms that live in the human intestines and can grow up to 3 metres (10 feet) in length. Treatment at that time was not very effective, so Doctor Meyers decided to try an unusual idea of his own.

He made what he called a 'tapeworm trap', a small metal cylinder attached to a length of tube. The trap was baited with food, and swallowed by the patient. When the tapeworm took the bait (like a fish) it was caught and held by a metal spring closure, then hauled out of the patient's intestine by the doctor. End of tapeworm.

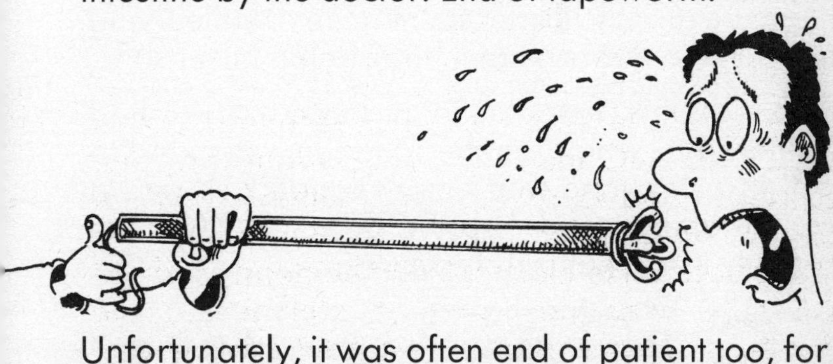

Unfortunately, it was often end of patient too, for most of Doctor Meyers' patients died, not of tapeworm infestation, but by choking on the tapeworm trap . . .

The Failed Five

In September 1987, in Manchester, northern England, a daring raid was planned on a building society office in the city centre. A five-man gang planned to steal thousands of pounds in cash as security men delivered it to the building. It was a very simple plan that just couldn't fail – or so the men thought . . .

The gang drove to the office, jumped out of their car to hold up the security guards – and found out that they had arrived five minutes too late. The guards – and the money – were safely inside the building. Still determined to get their hands on the cash, the men tried to force the steel doors with sticks, but failed miserably. Then they saw the parked security truck and, thinking that there might be money inside, spent quite a while trying to open the doors. Again, they failed miserably.

After all this time, quite a large crowd had gathered to watch, so the failed five decided to call it a day, and fled empty-handed. 'It was a typical amateur job,' said a detective. 'And the security truck was empty anyway . . .'

John's Commentary Hit a Snag(ge)

A traditional rowing race is held every year on the River Thames in England, between teams from Oxford and Cambridge universities. Large crowds gather to watch, and the event is broadcast on radio and telelvision. The race that took place in 1949 was a really close contest, and radio commentator John Snagge got very excited. 'It's a very close race,' he said. 'I can't see who is in the lead, but it's either Oxford . . . or Cambridge.' In a two-boat race it would be, wouldn't it?

A Tall Story

A sneak thief stole lots of cricket clothes and bats from a parked car in Manchester, northern England, in September 1987. Maybe he was a keen sportsman. He'd also have to be a tall sportsman – for the equipment belonged to West Indian cricketer Joel Garner, who stands 2.06 metres (6 feet 9 inches) high!

Every Home Should Have One

In March 1981, *The Sunday Times* newspaper, based in London, England, ran a light-hearted competition to find the best new inventions. Finalists included a dimmer switch to be used inside a fridge, so the milk cartons could enjoy subdued lighting, and, to reverse the trend towards smaller and smaller microchips, a house-sized calculator powered by an enormous maxichip.

Another idea was for see-through yashmaks to be worn by Arab women, waterproof teabags that produced a tasteless, colourless drink, and a silent alarm clock that didn't disturb the owner with a loud noise, but simply waved a flag. . .

A M Meadows suggested a blow-up plastic dart board for campers, and Frank Muir wanted to see extra-large bicycle clips to be worn around the thighs when cycling in shorts! Needless to say, every one of these ideas failed to find a commercial outlet . . .

Sssssshhhhhhh. . .

Marcel Marceau released a record album called *The Best of Marcel Marceau,* but it failed to sell many copies. Why? Each side of the album featured 20 minutes of complete silence followed by 20 seconds of polite applause. Mr Marceau is a French mime artist . . .

Royal Beefburgers

The wedding of Queen Elizabeth II (then Princess Elizabeth) on 20 November, 1947, was an important state occasion in Britain. Tens of thousands of people gathered to watch the pageantry in London, and millions more around the world listened to radio commentaries on the ceremony. However, one American commentator failed to convey the magic of the occasion when he described the Yeomen of the Guard in their ceremonial costumes. 'Near me is one of the special King's police in his Tudor finery,' he told listeners. 'These men are called Beefburgers, and each one holds a Halibut in his hand.' He failed to realize that the Beefburgers were really Beefeaters, and they held long-handled spears called 'Halberds', not fish!

Pepsodent Took a (Tooth)pasting

In the 1950s, the Pepsodent Company of America decided to launch their successful toothpaste in a new market: south-east Asia. Meetings were held, and advertising executives spent many weeks and thousands of dollars deciding on an advertising campaign to launch the product. Finally, they decided to use the slogan that had worked so well for them in America: 'You'll wonder where the yellow went when you brush your teeth with Pepsodent'. Posters went up, television adverts were broadcast, and full-page adverts appeared in newspapers. But hardly any orders arrived, and a top Pepsodent executive flew to Asia to find out why.

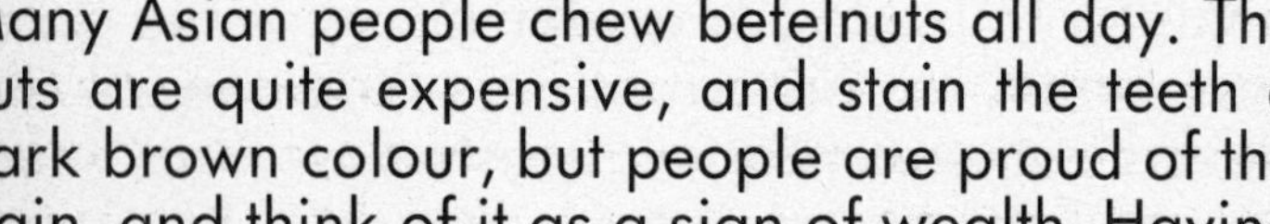

He soon found out why the slogan had flopped. Many Asian people chew betelnuts all day. The nuts are quite expensive, and stain the teeth a dark brown colour, but people are proud of the stain, and think of it as a sign of wealth. Having white teeth means that you are poor, so toothpaste that offered white teeth was not exactly popular. The advertising campaign was a flop, and Pepsodent quietly withdrew their toothpaste from the market.

Now You See It. . .

Percival Lowell was a famous astronomer based at the observatory in Flagstaff, Arizona, USA. He was a very well-respected scientist, and caused a lot of interest when, in 1908, he announced that he had made a new discovery about the planet Mars. There were canals on Mars, he said, (about 500 of them) – red canals that seemed to move, though he couldn't quite explain how. He drew detailed maps of the canals, and they appeared in books all over the world.

Unfortunately, Lowell's new discovery was a flop – there are no canals on Mars, either red or any other colour. But how had he 'seen' them through his microscope? Lowell was found to be suffering from a rare eye disease where the patient can see the tiny red veins in his or her own eyes. What Lowell had seen were not canals on Mars, but the tiny veins in his eyes . . .

Z-Rays Zapped

George Zerrett lived and worked in Chicago, USA, in the 1940s. He announced one day that he had perfected an amazing new device called the Z-ray applicator, which could cure just about any ailment from blisters to bunions. Zerrett claimed that his applicator was filled with precious atomic liquid, a by-product of heavy water and the atom bomb.

The Z-ray applicator sold in large numbers until people started to complain that their corns and chilblains showed no signs of improvement. No wonder – the Zerrett Z-ray applicator contained nothing more amazing than plain, ordinary, Chicago drinking-water! Sales of the device plummeted, and the Z-ray applicator was branded a fraudulent flop.

Quiet, Please!

A television presenter called Natalie Anglesey was filing a filmed report for the British Broadcasting Corporation in the summer of 1987. Her subject was the Lake District, an area in north-west England famed for its majestic mountain scenery, its peaceful lakes, and its get-away-from-it-all atmosphere. Nata-

lie was being filmed on Lake Windermere, talking about the area as the perfect place to spend a quiet weekend, but still hadn't completed the piece after dozens and dozens of takes. She hadn't fluffed or forgotten her lines – her words about the calm atmosphere couldn't be heard over the noise of roaring boats that raced by every few seconds pulling water-skiers!

Fiasco in C Major

Felix Mendelssohn, the famous composer, failed miserably when he turned his hand to conducting in 1844. He admired Franz Schubert's work, and was to perform his *Great C Major Symphony* with the London Philharmonic Orchestra, the first time the work had been played in England. Rehearsals began, but soon the orchestra became restless. 'There's no tune,' they whispered. 'This is awful. What rubbish. No wonder it's not played more often.' After a few more minutes the whole orchestra laid down their instruments and left Mendelssohn, baton in hand, facing rows and rows of empty chairs. . .

The Chef With Egg on His Face

Business wasn't exactly booming at a small hotel in South Africa, so the chef decided to put some novelty dishes on the menu to bring in more customers. He tried out his first new dish on guests staying for breakfast. They had all tried hens' eggs, goose eggs – even duck eggs – but the chef was sure that none of them had eaten ostrich eggs! Waiters took several orders for boiled ostrich eggs, but the chef's idea flopped as the guests waited – and waited – and waited. He'd forgotten that ostrich eggs are about 30 times bigger than hens' eggs, and it takes a whole hour to boil them! By the time they were ready, the guests had all left. . .

Gambler Royal

King Henry VIII of England, who lived from 1491 to 1547, was a larger-than-life character who enjoyed music, feasting and gambling. But as a gambler, Henry was a flop – he once lost the bells of St Paul's Cathedral, in London, in a game of dice!

From Pet to Pest

This is a story about a little rabbit called Cottontail. She was owned by a boy called Teddy Hughes, and when he and his family started a new life in New South Wales, Australia, Cottontail went with them on the ship. For a while, she was the only rabbit in Australia, as rabbit were unknown there.

Soon after the Hughes family arrived, Cottontail escaped into the bush. She wasn't alone for long, though, for she had a litter of baby rabbits. That's when Cottontail proved a real failure as a pet, for those few rabbits bred and bred over a few years until the whole vast country was overrun with millions of them. That one rabbit had started a dynasty that threatened the livelihoods of thousands of farmers. . .

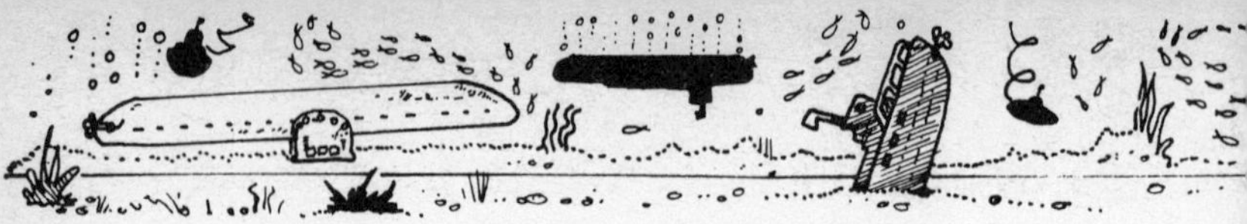

Substandard Submaries

During World War One, from 1914 to 1918, the British Admiralty decided to build a large flotilla of submarines to help the war effort. The submarines were huge – 100 metres (328 feet) long – and were steam-powered. They were to be called K-boats, and great things were expected of them. On paper the K-boats seemed like a good idea, but in water, they flopped miserably. One sprang a leak while still in dry dock, another ran aground in trials, and two K-boats rammed each other and sank. One K-boat caught fire on its first dive, and another travelled to the ocean bed – and got stuck there. The K-boat project was finally filed under 'failures', and was abandoned in 1918.

Jailer Failure

The biggest failure as a jailer has to be Monsieur Masset, who worked as a warder at the Versailles Prison, near Paris, France. In October 1926, he was on duty guarding the prison's main doors one very cold night, when he decided to leave his post and go to a nearby cafe for a cup of coffee. But Monsieur Masset was also lonely – so he woke up a prisoner, and took him to the cafe to keep him

company! Was the huge prison totally unguarded? No, of course not – Monsieur Masset had unlocked another prisoner, and left him on guard outside the main doors! Monsieur Masset's action was discovered, and he was fired on the spot.

Watch the Birdie!

Press photographers follow the British Royal Family all over the world in the hope of snapping them off-duty. One British cameraman followed Princess Alexandra when she went to Spain on her honeymoon, and thought he had a foolproof plan to get some good pictures. He climbed to the top of a tall tree overlooking her hideaway, and set up his camera in the top branches, hidden by leaves. Now all he had to do was wait.

He didn't have to wait long for the action to begin. Spanish police had watched him climbing the tree and setting up his camera, and before he took his first shot they quietly chopped down the tree. Down he came, camera and all!

The One-Night Flop

It was greeted as a very important find: a young man called William Henry Ireland had discovered a new and unknown play by William Shakespeare, the great English dramatist, in an old trunk. The discovery caused great excitement and the play, called *Vortigern and Rowena*, was put on stage at the Theatre Royal, Drury Lane, London, in 1796. The famous actor, John Kemble, took the title role, but soon after the performance started, the audience grew restless. The writing seemed like that of an amateur copying Shakespeare's style, and the actors were making fun of their lines. Kemble spoke in a very high voice that made the audience laugh every time he opened his mouth, and in a death scene, he accidentally fell, pulling down a curtain to reveal the 'corpse' running off stage! Kemble thought that the play was a fake, and wanted the audience to know it.

He was right. The play had been written by 19 year-old Ireland. His father was a keen Shakespearian scholar who dreamed of finding unknown works by the great man. To please him, William forged some letters, told his father he had found them, and enjoyed the fame when experts said they were genuine. William forged more documents and then became more ambitious, writing the five-act play.

That first performance of *Vortigern and Rowena* was also its last. The tragedy became a comic farce, fighting broke out in the theatre, and the curtain finally fell on one of history's most famous one-night flops. . .

Out Voted

In the Presidential elections held in Liberia, west Africa, in 1927, supporters of one candidate, Charles King, were determined that their man would win. So determined were they, that they rigged the election, and King was proclaimed President. But someone had got their sums wrong – King's 'majority' was more than 15 times greater than the total number of people who had voted!

That Sinking Feeling

George Garrett was a clergyman in Manchester, northern England. His interests were not all Biblical. He dreamed of building an underwater vessel, and formed The Garrett Submarine Navigation and Pneumataphore Company to produce Britain's first submarine. The 30-tonne, 13.7 metre (45 foot) cigar-shaped vessel was built in 1879, and Garrett had great hopes for *Resurgam* (meaning, 'I rise again'). She was steam-powered, and could, said Garrett, stay underwater for four hours.

The launch (funded partly by Garrett's congregation) was in 1880. Failure loomed from the start, when the crew became lost in Liverpool Bay and had to ask directions from a passing ship. *Resurgam* finally set out to sea, and submerged as planned. What wasn't planned was that she didn't rise again. She lies on the seabed to this day. Garrett left the church and died, penniless, in New York, USA, in 1902.

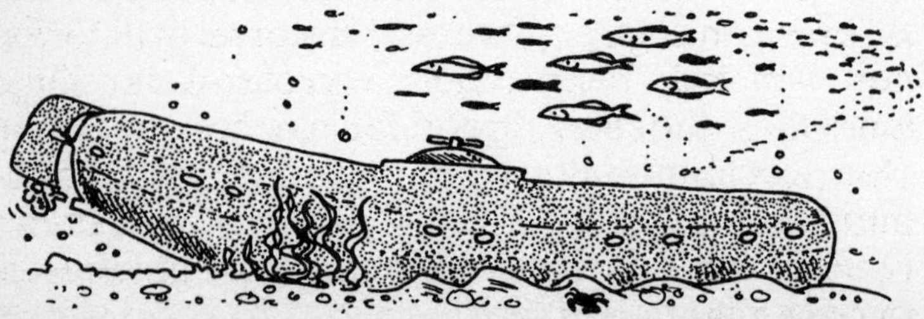

Get Out of That!

British woman, Yvonne Whittlesham, called herself The Psychic Escapologist. In April 1977, she announced that she would perform a remarkable stunt – she would drive a car at fast speeds over a 96 kilometre (60 mile) stretch of road – blindfolded! Roads were cleared, and a large crowd gathered to watch as Yvonne put on an iron blindfold guaranteed to block her vision completely. She climbed into her car, then drove for just over 1,00 metres (3,300 feet) in a straight line before crashing into the side of a barn. . . Some psychic!

It's a Knockout!

Ralph Walton was the boxing flop of 1946. He was fighting in Lewiston, Maine, USA, against Al Couture. Ralph was still adjusting his gumshield in his corner when the fight started. His opponent crossed the ring, landed one punch, and knocked him out cold. The fight lasted just ten-and-a-half seconds – and ten seconds were taken up by the referee's count, before Ralph Walton was declared unfit to continue.

A Suitable (Pillow)case for Treatment

In Riverside, California, USA, a thief planned to rob a big store. He lived in the area, so a good disguise was important. The thief had an idea – he would wear a pillowcase over his head. That way he could speak and be heard, but no one would see his face.

The plan started to go badly wrong when the thief forgot to cut eye holes in the pillowcase. He pulled it over his head outside the store, then crashed about inside. He failed to find his way to the cash desk, and a crowd gathered to watch as he stumbled around, knocking over displays and racks. The thief decided to give up and go home – but he couldn't find the way out. In a panic, the thief pulled off the pillowcase and ran for the door – but not before he had been recognized by a neighbour. . .

Clueless

A woman from the island of Fiji, in the Pacific Ocean, wrote to *The Times* newspaper in London in May 1966 to say that she had just completed the newspaper's cross-

word. The crossword is notoriously difficult, but the lady failed to win a prize for her efforts – the puzzle had appeared in April 1932. It had taken her more than 34 years to solve the puzzle!

It Wasn't Like This in the Movies

An American tourist staying at the Metropole Hotel in Moscow, USSR, was worried that his room might be bugged. He didn't like the idea of anyone spying on him, and decided to search his room. He'd seen how it was done in the movies, so he carefully checked under the bed, inside the desk and behind the mirror. He lifted the rug – and found a small brass plate screwed to the floor. Thinking it was a bugging device, he started to unscrew it.

Unfortunately, as a bug-spotter, the tourist was a spectacular failure – the brass plate supported the huge glass chandelier that hung in the great ballroom below. . .

Scoop

In April 1983, the German magazine *Stern* announced that it had pulled off a great scoop: reporters had discovered the previously unknown diaries of the Nazi wartime dictator, Adolf Hitler. They had paid $3,000,000 for the secret diaries, and planned to publish them all over the world.

But were the diaries genuine? *The Times* newspaper group of London, who planned to publish the diaries in Britain, decided to find out, and called in Lord Dacre, a respected historian and an expert on Nazi history. The diaries, 60 large volumes in all, were pronounced genuine. One reason why Lord Dacre believed they were genuine was that he couldn't imagine anyone going to the trouble of forging such a vast amount of hand-written material. The diaries really were those of Adolf Hitler, he stated.

But Lord Dacre had failed to spot a fake. Soon after, the diaries were found to be the work of the forger Konrad Kujau, who had written the diaries in just three weeks. . .

A Code in de Toes

Scientists have searched for a cure for the common cold for many years, without any real success. Hopes were raised in 1971 when Doctor Schwartz, working in Israel, announced that he had found a cure. No drugs or medicines were needed – sufferers were simply treated with intense cold. The whole body didn't need to be iced – just the undersides of the patient's big toes! The treatment could take place at home, with the patient putting his big toes into a freezer. The idea was a failure – patients who tried it out just ended up with a cold in the toes, as well as a cold in the nose!

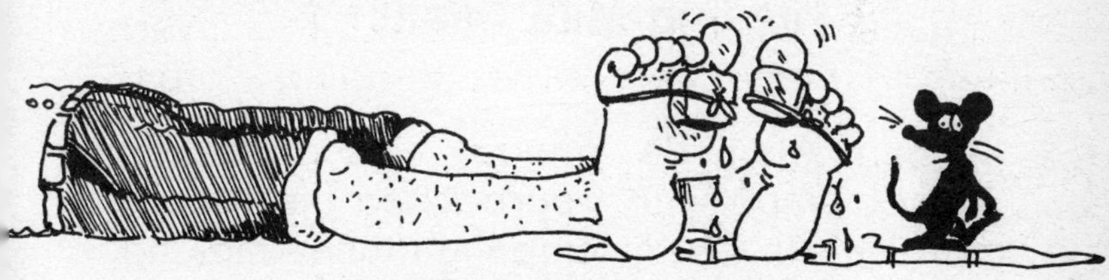

Exhibit Number Eleven

The catalogue of an art exhibition held at the Serpentine Gallery in Kensington Gardens, London, England, in 1983, read 'Number 11 is a new, interesting and unusual work.' It was that all right – a tray of animal droppings. Needless to say, the exhibition was a flop.

1,2,3,4,5,6,7. . . 8!

Georg Hegel, the German scientist and philosopher, published a paper in 1807. In it he stated very forcefully that there could be no more than seven planets in the solar system. He claimed absolute proof, and staked his reputation on his theory. Just one week later the eighth planet was discovered!

The Con-Man Count

Count Alain de Villegas was a Belgian nobleman who approached the French government with a very tempting money-making scheme. He told them that he was certain that there was oil under French soil, and what was more, he could pin-point its exact locations. The French economy of the 1970s was not healthy, and the millions of francs that oil sales can raise would have been very welcome. President Giscard d'Estaing studied the Count's proposals, liked them, and agreed that the government would finance his scheme.

The Count, with the help of Italian scientist Aldo Bonassoli, demonstrated his oil-finding machine. Mounted on a plane, the machine literally sniffed out oil deposits thousands of metres below, and marked them on maps. At enormous cost, the machine was developed, mounted on a plane, and flown across France for hundreds of hours. When it landed, the Count handed over maps of the country, with the oil deposits clearly marked.

Oil rigs were erected, and drilling started in 1976, but three years later not one drop of oil had been found. People started to feel uneasy – Villegas and Bonassoli had been given millions of francs, but where was the oil they had promised to find? The sniffing machine was seized and inside it police found – maps, a xerox copying machine, and some felt-tip pens! The Count had marked the amazing maps by hand!

The French government had been tricked into giving the Count some 300,000,000 francs. As a scheme to make Villegas and Bonassoli rich, the machine was a great success, but as an oil-finder, it was a spectacular flop. . .

Watch the Birdies!

A keen walker decided to spend a week walking along the scenic Dorset coastal path in southern England. He pitched his tent one fine evening as darkness fell, and went to sleep.

He was woken up by thousands of birds as dawn broke. He knew the area was rich in bird life, but this was amazing – the air was filled with birds of all kinds. The walker crawled from his tent – and found out why. He had camped right on the edge of a huge refuse dump, and the birds had all come to scavenge there on rotting food.

Oil Gone

When the oil boom hit Scotland, someone had a bright idea – at least it seemed like a bright idea at the time. There would be work for many oil rig construction workers in Argyll, on Scotland's west coast, but nowhere for them to live, so a purpose-built 'village' was constructed at Polphail. Many millions of pounds were spent on building rooms, meeting areas, entertainment rooms and a 500-seat restaurant. But before the buildings were completed, the construction work was moved elsewhere, and the new village was never lived in.

Brabazon Gone

After World War Two, Lord Brabazon of Tara was appointed to head a committee to plan the future of the British aircraft industry. After much deliberation, the committee decided to build the Brabazon, a plane they hoped was large enough to fly anywhere in the world, yet slow enough to take off and land on primitive air strips. It sounded good on paper. . .

The reality was a little different. The Brabazon was certainly slow, so slow that it could be outflown by much earlier, almost primitive planes. And it was large – so heavy that the plane's frame cracked under its own weight. Before the plane was completed, the new jet engine was developed, completely outdating the Brabazon's piston-powered engines. The Brabazon was scrapped. It had cost over £12,000,000, but had never carried a passenger.

Audience – What Audience?

A theatre in the town of Grantham, in eastern England, was the setting for a performance of a comedy play called *Bag*. But the performance – in December 1983 – was a miserable and very quiet failure, for the only people in the theatre were the members of the cast.

It Works Like Clockwork

In September 1934, *The Times* newspaper carried reports of a new type of Japanese car. Instead of a petrol engine, the car was powered by clockwork. The new idea was a big flop, though, as someone had to run behind the car and wind it up every few hundred yards. It didn't catch on. . .

Mission Impossible

Mathias Rust was an idealistic young man. The 19 year-old West German was disappointed when the summit meeting between Soviet leader Mikhail Gorbachev and American president Ronald Reagan broke up without agreement in October 1986, and decided that he had to do something to publicise the search for peace between east and west. He decided to fly on a peace mission to Russia.

In May 1987, without permission, he flew his tiny plane from Helsinki, Finland, across 800 kilometres (500 miles) of Russian territory completely undetected by Soviet defence systems, until he reached Moscow. To the amazement of passers-by, he landed his plane in the middle of Red Square outside the Kremlin, the government's headquarters, and told soldiers that he had arrived on a private peace mission.

Sadly, Mathias' mission was as much a failure as the summit meeting. He was arrested, tried, and sentenced to four years hard labour by the Russian courts.

No Thanks

The biggest flop as a gift has to be the one offered to comedy star Lillian Russell in 1919 by a great fan of hers, Mr Schuyler of Philadelphia, USA. The gift was worth thousands of dollars, said Mr Schuyler, and Miss Russell told him she would be pleased to accept it. She wasn't too pleased when the gift was delivered – it was a gold-trimmed coffin. Mr Schuyler was an undertaker. . .

Doggone

The police force in Manchester, northern England, held a special course for dog-handlers in September 1987. Six policemen were chosen to attend the course, but four of them failed before they had even started. Why? The force had only two dogs available. . .

Walking on Water

In 1899, Professor Miller announced that he would travel from America to England. Nothing very unusual about that, you might say, except that the professor intended to *walk* across the mighty Atlantic Ocean. Huge crowds gathered to watch as he set off from the East River in Manhattan, New York, ready for the epic journey. He strapped his feet into strange canoe-shaped shoes about 1.2 metres (4 feet) long, waved goodbye, and set off. He covered a few hundred metres before the shoes became waterlogged and he sank slowly under the water, his epic journey an epic flop.

Yo, Ho, Ho!

The least successful pirate must be Ernest Hargreaves, an Englishman who called himself Commander of the Pirates in 1920, and announced that he was about to terrorise the world. Sadly for Ernest, his reign of terror was short-lived. He was sent to prison, not for stealing treasure or roaming the high seas, but for stealing a bicycle. . .

Crowned!

King Edward VII of England was crowned in Westminster Abbey, London, in 1902. The Archbishop of Canterbury was very old and frail, and when the time came for him to place the heavy Imperial Crown on the new King's head, it looked as if he might not manage it. He did – but the crown was on back to front!

Dangerous Sports

David Kirke and Hugo Spower are members of the Dangerous Sports Club based in London, England. On 19 August, 1986, they climbed inside a huge 20 metre (65 feet) high inflatable PVC balloon and began to 'walk' it along the River Thames. They planned to use the balloon to cross the English Channel between England and France later, and this was their first practice run.

Their practice run came to a watery end when, after just five minutes, the balloon popped and slowly deflated. Their 'dangerous sport' had become just one big, wet, flop.

Double Your Money

There were just two men in the county jail in Eagle, Texas, USA – confidence trickster Victor Lustig and the Sheriff, Quentin Richards. The two men chatted, and the Sheriff told his prisoner that he had a problem. He worked as sheriff *and* tax collector, and had pocketed $30,000 of government money. The auditors were due to visit, and the Sheriff thought he would end up behind the bars of his own jail.

'No problem,' said Lustig. 'I happen to have an amazing machine that will duplicate bank notes. You simply feed in a one-hundred dollar bill, the machine copies it, returns the original, plus a new one, and you double your money. Let me escape and you can have it.' The Sheriff agreed, stole another $25,000 to copy, and allowed Lustig to escape.

In secret he fed the first bank note into the machine and waited. It came out the other side, but no copy emerged, of course. The machine was as big a failure as the Sheriff was a jailer. . .

Anything You Can Do. . .

Major Jim Howard set out for America in September 1987, determined to beat Virgin boss Richard Branson's transatlantic hot-air balloon record, set up earlier that year. He believed he could make the journey from America to England in a faster time, but had to accept that his attempt was a flop. In fact it didn't really get off the ground: weather conditions were bad, and Major Howard was forced to cancel his balloon flight and return to Britain on a Boeing 767. . .

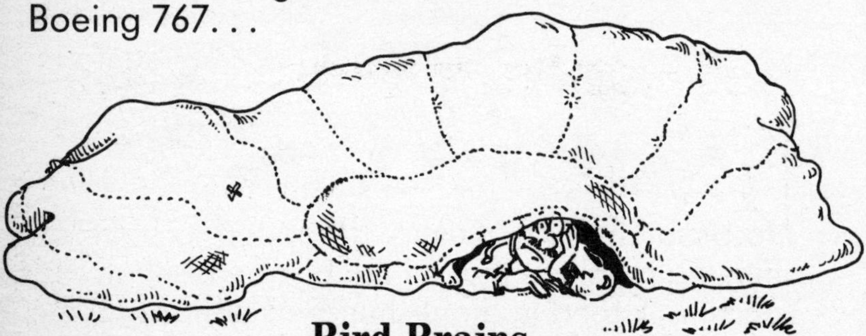

Bird Brains

Pigeon racing is a popular hobby in many parts of the world. Pigeons released hundreds of miles from their home lofts will somehow find their way back, often in awful weather conditions. The biggest flops in the pigeon racing world have to be the members of the Alternative Pigeon Fanciers Association of

Hazel Grove, near Manchester, northern England. They are lucky if their pigeons cover 46 metres (150 feet). Why? The flying flops are fake pigeons powered by elastic bands. . .

A Foggy Day, in Pittsburg Town. . .

Pittsburg, California, on America's west coast, was a city often troubled by thick fog. In the 1920s, the city's administrators became concerned about the fog problem, and decided to do something about it. After a lot of thought, they decided on a plan, and carried it out. They poured many thousands of litres of oil into the river that ran by the city. The idea was that the oil would prevent moisture forming in the air, and therefore no fog would form. The idea was an absolute flop, and Pittsburg was as foggy as ever. Worse than that, the city's administrators had given themselves another problem, for the oil badly polluted the river. . .

Gold Fever

In 1931, a German called Franz Tausend announced that he could 'make' gold. Now, as everyone knows, gold is found naturally and cannot be manufactured, but Herr Tausend persuaded people that his experiments had been successful. The German government was penniless after World War One, and desperate to refill the banks, so they agreed to pay him handsomely for his 'raw materials'.

Herr Tausend set to work. His theory was simple: every substance has a natural resonance, he explained; when the right note is struck, base metals turn to gold! Tausend worked for many weeks, well supplied with money, but at the end of that time he had 'made' just one piece of gold, and a few grains. His methods had failed miserably, and he was branded a fake and sent to prison for three years.

Bang, Bang, You're Dead!

In the 17th-century, the Swedish Royal Court was overrun by fleas, and Queen Christina hated them. By 1626, she was so fed up with the nasty insects that she offered a large reward to anyone who could help her get rid of them. Powders and potions were all tried without success, then the Queen was given a tiny cannon just 10 centimetres (4 inches) long. It fired tiny shot, and the idea was that the Queen would fire it at the fleas, blowing them to bits. But the inventor had forgotten one important thing about fleas – they are champion jumpers. When the Queen fired at them, they simply jumped out of the way, and fled. That's probably what the inventor did when Queen Christina turned the mini-cannon on him. . .

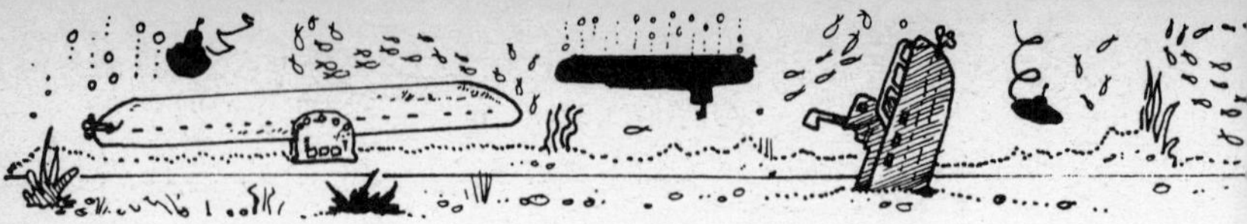

Doom and Gloom

Dora Ashbough was prone to depression and gloomy thoughts. She planned to take her own life when things got too much for her, and carried poison around with her for more than 20 years. Finally, in 1930, in San Francisco, USA, she took the poison. But her suicide attempt failed miserably – after all those years, the poison had lost its power, and was quite harmless. Dora had good reason to be depressed. . .

Mouse Hunter Extraordinaire!

As well as a mouse-hunter, Madame Fauganelle also became a very successful demolition expert. In 1935, at her home near Bordeaux in south-west France, she spotted a mouse as it ran into a hole under the kitchen sink. Deciding to catch the mouse, Madame took a red-hot poker from the fire and thrust it into the hole. What she didn't know was that her husband used the hole as a storage place for his explosive powder and gun cartridges. As the

poker touched the cartridges, there was a huge explosion that reduced the house to a heap of rubble and splintered wood. 'You have ruined our house,' said Monsieur Fauganelle on his return.

'Ah, yes,' said Madame Fauganelle, who survived the explosion, standing amidst the ruined house. 'But I *did* kill that mouse!'

Barchilar of Artes

John Smith of Reading, in southern England, thought he'd hit on a great money-making scheme. He would offer degree certificates from his own private 'university' for a fee of £100. Students could impress future employers with their qualifications, without having had to do even one hour's study. But the fake degrees were spotted right away, and Smith didn't sell one. Smith's problem was that he couldn't spell, and his 'Digrees in Engleesh Liteertur' failed to impress anyone.

Nessie 1, Fireman 0

Ever since Saint Columba recorded the first sighting of the Loch Ness monster in the year 565 AD, people have tried – and failed – to prove its existence. Eye-witness accounts and photographs have been produced over the years since then, but the monster (or monsters) remains elusive. Loch Ness, in northern Scotland, is Britain's longest lake at 38.99 kilometres (24.3 miles), and is also one of the deepest, and hundreds of people have tried to solve the mystery of its inky waters.

A group of firemen tried to lure the monster – nicknamed Nessie – from its water home in 1975. Believing that the monster was male, they reasoned that only a female monster would lure him to the surface so that they could photograph him – or even catch him. Female monsters being thin on the ground, they set about building one in papier-mâché. The finished female was 9 metres (30 feet) long, painted green, and had long eyelashes. Two firemen sat inside her to steer and, with an outboard motor fixed to her tail, she was launched on the Loch.

Though the firemen made what they thought were female monster mating-calls, the lure failed miserably. Not only did the male monster fail to show himself, after a few kilometres, the

outboard motor went crazy, and the female monster raced backwards across the Loch before crashing into a jetty and ending up a wet, crumpled heap. Better luck next time. . .

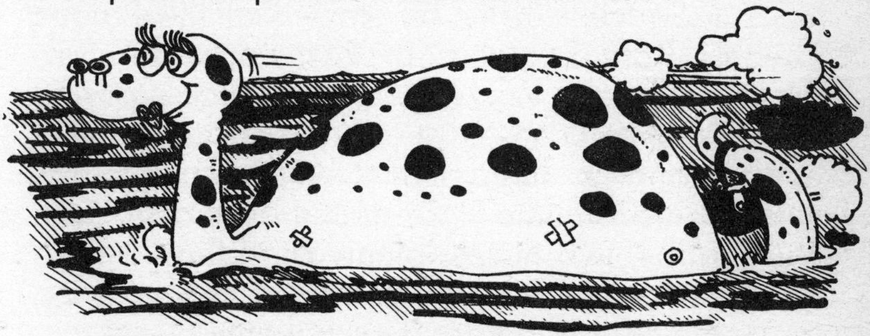

Take Twenty-Nine? Oh, Forget It!

The biggest failure as a performer in a television advertising commercial has to be the British actress Pat Coombs. Hired to provide the voice-over on a commercial for a new brand of breakfast cereal in 1973, she learned her lines and turned up at the studio to record them. Take one – and Pat got her lines right, until she came to say the name of the product, which she just couldn't remember. Take two was the same – as soon as Pat had to name the cereal she dried up. The same things happened on takes three, four, five – and the rest. In all Pat failed 28 times, at which point everyone gave up and went home. The commercial was never completed, and the product was taken off the market soon after.

Curtain Up

A review called *Fig Leaves and Apple Sauce,* due to be staged at the Palace Theatre, Bath, England, in 1944, flopped before the curtain rose. Why? A railway truck carrying all the show's props, scenery and costumes went astray, and in its place a whole orchestra's musical instruments were delivered. Faced with two pianos, two harps, plenty of violins, but no costumes or scenery, the company had to bring down the curtain before it even went up. . .

Just Call Me Fingers

Robert Schumann was a young musical prodigy. He had natural talent, and played the piano very well, but he didn't like practising. He was playing one day in 1832 when he had a bright idea, something that would take all the strain out of practice sessions. He made himself a 'finger tormentor' that raised his forefinger from the keyboard, making the other fingers work harder. Schumann was delighted with the gadget, but in a few months it had damaged his hands so badly that he was never able to play the piano again.

Shoot Over The Money Or I'll Hold!

The biggest flop as a bank robber has to be the Irishman called Patrick O'Reilly who tried to rob a London bank in the 1960s. He put his hand under his jacket and walked up to a cashier, threatening to shoot her if she didn't hand over all the money in her desk. Realizing that the man wasn't carrying a real gun, the cashier calmly refused, and the would-be robber became very angry. 'You aren't being very helpful,' he said. 'I'm going to have to report you to the manager.'

'You have the right to do that, sir,' said the cashier, taking a piece of paper and a pen from her desk. 'May I have your name and address for the complaint form?' Without thinking, O'Reilly gave the cashier his full name and address and left the bank empty-handed, realizing that his plan had failed miserably. He was even more upset when he found the police waiting to arrest him when he got home. . .

His Master's Voice

Thomas Edison, the American inventor of the phonograph, came up with a very unusual sewing machine powered by the human voice. The machine worked quite well, but at no small cost to the machinist, who had to shout very loudly for as long as the machine worked. Voices flagged, and the machine was a flop.

A Nutty Idea

In the aftermath of World War Two, which ended in 1945, there was a great shortage of food. There were millions of people in war-torn Europe who did not have enough to eat. In 1946, Great Britain's Minister of Food, John Strachey, thought up a scheme he hoped would solve the problem. His plan was to grow huge amounts of groundnuts (peanuts rich in valuable protein) in Africa. Strachey chose more than 1,214,100 hectares (3,000,000 acres) of land in Tanganyika, Kenya and Rhodesia for the project, and planting started on a vast scale.

Right from the start there were problems. The soil was poor, the weather conditions unsuitable, and there was not enough water. In one area where there was no water, engineers heard of natural springs in a nearby pool, and planned to dam them and pipe water to the groundnut fields. But African workers were reluctant to help – the pool was the special place of the Mganga, or witch doctor, and they didn't want to anger him. Engineers went to the Mganga and he agreed that they could use the water. He charged them a fee of one shilling (now five pence) and for that even threw in a magic spell to guarantee the safety of the dam!

Despite more than £40,000,000 being spent on the groundnut scheme – including the Mganga's shilling – the whole idea was a spectacular flop. Hardly one groundnut was harvested, and Strachey's idea was one of the worst agricultural failures ever. He was forced to abandon his nutty scheme in 1947.

Chop, Chop!

Robert Liston was a Scottish surgeon who was famed for the speed of his operations. But in 1814, his career fell from fame to failure when he amputated a patient's leg in less than a minute – but cut off three of his assistant's fingers was well!

Suck, Don't Blow

In about 1900, an American inventor tried to sell a new machine that he claimed would remove dust from carpets. The first vacuum cleaner? Not quite – this machine didn't suck up the dust, it just blew it around the room. Needless to say, the idea was a huge flop.

Penguin Power

A safari park was taken over by a new team of managers with bright, modern ideas. One of the things they didn't like was the penguin pool. It was dark, dull, and gloomy, and the managers decided to repaint it in bright, colourful designs and patterns so that it would look more attractive and encourage more visitors. The penguins were moved out of the pool, and when the paint had dried they were returned to their multicoloured new home. Next morning, the penguins were all found lying flat on their backs, apparently lifeless, and a penguin expert was called in. He took one look at the bright, patterned pool and explained what had happened. The penguins were from a bleak area of Argentina, South America, where the only scenery was dull, grey rocks. They had all been stunned and temporarily blinded by the bright colours and patterns in the pool. As soon as the pool was repainted in dull grey the penguins made a full recovery.

Has Anyone Got a Map?

In 1964, revolutionaries organized a coup to overthrow the Italian government in Rome. The ringleaders brought in supporters from all over Italy and let them loose on the outskirts of the city. They were to stampede to the centre of the city, but unfortunately, most of the rioters were not from Rome, and soon became lost in the maze of back streets. No more than 100 made it to the meeting point, and the coup fizzled out. The coup was such a disaster that the government didn't even realize it had happened until one of the organizers told them five years later. . .

Fail Safe

Would-be bank robbers failed miserably when they tried to open a safe inside a bank in Munkebo, in Denmark. They carefully set explosive charges, lit them, and were knocked to the ground by the massive explosion that followed. The bank was demolished, and the whole building reduced to rubble. The only thing that wasn't damaged was – the safe!

Film Flop

Heaven's Gate holds the record as the film world's greatest flop. The film lost more than $57,000,000, and sent United Artists out of business as an independent studio.

Pride Comes Before a . . . Forgery

Elias Mutumbe was a crook from Kenya in Africa, who was a very skilled forger. He took a lot of trouble to get his work just right, and was very proud of his talents. He forged some bank notes, using the finest paper, and inks that were identical to the real ones, and spent many hours copying the detailed engraving. He was delighted when he printed the first forged note – it was almost identical to the real ones. But Elias's forgeries were an immediate failure, and he was arrested as soon as he tried to pay for something with his fake bank notes. Why? Elias was so proud of his work that instead of the head of the Kenyan president on the bank notes, he had etched a picture of himself!

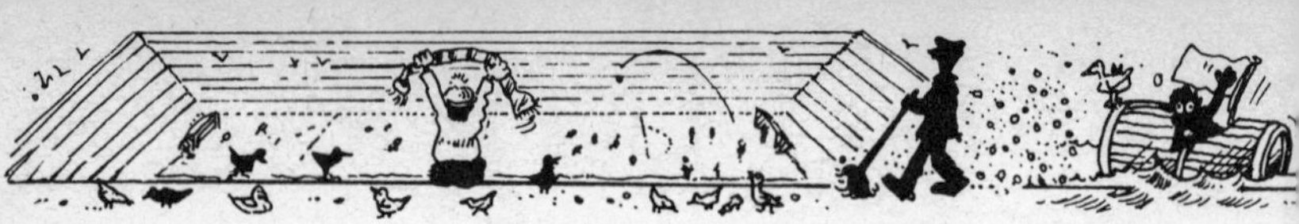

If at First You Don't Succeed. . .

Try, try, try again. That was the motto of Miriam Hargrave of Wakefield, Yorkshire, in northern England, who failed her driving test no less than 39 times over a period of eight years. Much to her relief, she passed her test at the 40th attempt in August 1970.

Another determined failure was Fannie Turner of Little Rock, Arkansas, USA. She took – and failed – her written driving test 103 times before finally passing in 1978, aged 75.

A Bullet-Proof Scheme

People living in Miami, Florida, USA, grew worried about the wave of muggings, robberies and violent crime on the streets. Some were so afraid of being shot that they hardly ever left their homes. One big store in the city decided that they would cash in on the fears of residents, and advertised bullet-proof vests

for sale. But the vests were a flop, and the store sold hardly any. Why? Perhaps it was the advertising idea the store chose. 'Buy a bullet-proof vest from us,' they promised, 'and if it doesn't work, we'll give you one million dollars.' As the residents of Miami reasoned: if the bullet-proof vest doesn't work, who's going to be around to enjoy the million dollars?

Frozen Bacon

On a freezing cold winter's day, back in March 1626, the famous English scientist and philosoper, Francis Bacon, left his London home to conduct a simple experiment. He wondered if ice would slow down food decay, and wanted to put his idea to the test. He took a chicken and stuffed it with snow, then a few days later he ate the chicken meat. Unfortunately Francis never did find out if his early tries at refrigeration were successful – he caught a cold in the snow, then died from typhoid soon after. He had presumably caught it from eating the frozen chicken meat. . .

Always Leave a Calling Card

Train robber Neil David of Birmingham, England, used a simple skeleton key to open and rob mail vans. His last robbery turned into a real flop, though, when he was carrying off some mail sacks. He dropped his wallet inside the mail van, but didn't notice and set off for his home, congratulating himself on another successful raid. The police soon arrested him, for in his wallet in the mail van they found David's full name, his address – and even his photograph!

Dinosaur Dupes Diggers

At Tetouan, Morocco, on the north coast of Africa, workers discovered some strange objects when they were working in the fields in 1930. Experts were called in, and spent a long time studying the objects. Finally, they announced that the objects were the bones of a rare dinosaur that had been extinct for thousands of years. People came from far and near to look at the skeleton, and the remains were hailed a major archaeological find.

But the important find turned into an embarrassing flop when one expert looked even closer at the 'bones' and said that they were not the remains of a dinosaur, but bits of an old haymaking machine that had been buried in the earth for many years. The dinosaur's 'ribs' were really just the teeth of the rake!

The Kiss of Death

After a traditional wedding ceremony in China, the young couple went on to their reception. In a quiet moment they slipped away, sat on a sofa together, and kissed. But the groom kissed his bride so hard and for so long that when relatives went to look for them, they were found still sitting on the sofa, unconscious. They were taken to hospital, where the groom recovered, but sadly the bride died. She had been kissed to death.

First Stop Boulogne, Next Stop – Europe!

In 1981, Mr and Mrs Eltham decided to travel by ferry from Dover, England, to Boulogne, in France, for the day. Their few hours in the small French town were a great success, but when the time came for them to return to England, success turned to failure. . .

The Elthams didn't speak French, and couldn't read French road or street signs. They wandered around for a while then, realizing they'd missed the ferry, went to the railway station. They decided to travel by train to the French capital, Paris, and to travel home from there. They got on the Paris-bound train, but got off in another country – Luxembourg!

They took a train back to Paris, fell asleep on the long journey and woke up, not in Paris, but in yet another country – Switzerland! Swiss police took them over the border into France. Finally they reached Paris and caught a train for Boulogne. Unfortunately, the train they boarded took them to one more country – Germany!

They were sent back across the French border, and exasperated police drove them across the country to make sure they reached Boulogne. They finally got home weeks after they had set out, tired, penniless and dirty. As a European tour, the trip had succeeded, but as a day trip to France it has to be rated as the failure of all time.

He Picked the Wrong Pocket

A British newspaper, *The Times*, carried a story in its issue, dated 11 November, 1946, about an attempted robbery by a pick-pocket in London's Tottenham Court Road. Evidently, a thief had put his hand into the bulging pocket of a well-dressed man and pulled out, not a wallet, but a snake! The pickpocket had yelled, dropped the snake and run off empty-handed, a feeble failure. The snake was not dangerous, and belonged to a magician.

I Did Sail the Atlantic, Honest!

Eric Peters of Littlehampton, on the south-east coast of England, didn't have a job, but wanted to do something with his time, so he spent two years building a small barrel-shaped boat from bits and pieces. Then he decided to sail his boat, the *Toniky-Nou,* not just around the coast, but right across the mighty Atlantic Ocean. He set off from the Canary Islands and spent 46 days and nights in the tiny boat, which was just 1.79 metres (5 feet 10½ inches) long, living on a diet of nuts, olive oil and tiny sips of water. He completed the voyage in 1983, landing at Guadaloupe, Mexico. Then he travelled back to England. Now Eric hadn't told many people about his planned voyage, and he certainly didn't have press or TV coverage, so when he reached home and told people what he'd done, they refused to believe him. 'Tell us another one,' they said.

Belly Flop

In 1920, in a smart restaurant in Paris, France, a new dish appeared on the menu – roast lion. The lion, called Mascotte, had had an accident and had to be shot, but its trainer, Monsieur Marcel, didn't want to waste the expensive animal, so had him served at a meal for circus performers. But the new dish was a flop – diners reported that lion tastes *awful!*

It All Depends on Your Point of View

When the Museum of Modern Art in New York, USA, exhibited a painting by the French painter Henri Matisse in 1961, many thousands of people went to see it. *Le Bateau* was a popular exhibit, but the whole show became something of a flop when, after 47 days, a visitor pointed out that the painting had been hung upside down. . . No one else had noticed!

Snap, Crackle, Flop

In 1928, Herr von Opel announced that his revolutionary new 'rocket car' would be used in an attempt to better the world land speed record. Spectators gathered to watch the attempts at a 6 kilometre (4 mile) track near Hanover, Germany. Rockets filled with explosive powder were ignited by a mechanic, and the car snapped, crackled, and disappeared in a huge ball of flames and smoke. When the smoke cleared, the crowd saw that the car had travelled just a few yards along the track, and even the confident Herr von Opel had to admit that the record attempt had failed miserably. The car's 'pilot', a cat, was never seen again. . .

Here Today, Gone Tomorrow

The Knightsbridge Safe Deposit Centre in London, England, advertised itself as the safest place for people to store their valuables. All the floors were 3.7 metres (12 feet) thick, guards watched television monitors of the building for 24 hours a day, and amazingly sensitive

electronic devices picked up the slightest sound or movement. Those people who owned safe deposit boxes had to key in a personal computer-code number before they could get in – or out. People were impressed, and soon all the centre's boxes were filled.

But success turned to failure overnight. In July 1987, the centre was broken into and goods worth more than £40,000,000 were stolen. . .

A Load of Old Bull

A French farmer got really fed up when nudists from a nearby camp took a short cut across his field to get to the beach. Then one day he thought up a brilliant way to stop them – or so he thought. He went to market and bought two dozen of the meanest, most ferocious bulls he could find and let them loose in the field. Then he hid in a bush and watched as the first nudists arrived and started to walk across his field, expecting the bulls to charge at any second. But the bulls took no notice of the nudists. The irate farmer went to a veterinary surgeon, who explained that without clothes, people just appear to bulls as fellow dumb animals. The farmer's plan had failed miserably, for though the bulls charged him, they ignored the nudists!

All Smash, No Grab

A thief planned to rob a large Hollywood jewellery store. He didn't make any clever plans or subtle schemes, he just decided to hurl a brick through the main window and grab as much as he could. What he didn't know, though, was that the window was made from special shatter-proof strengthened glass. The thief hurled the brick, which bounced back off the glass window and hit him on the head – hard. The blow flattened the thief, and he was still lying outside the store when police officers arrived to arrest him. Well, it seemed like a good idea at the time. . .

O'Carroll's Folly

Mr O'Carroll of Dublin, Ireland, tried – and failed – to sell his house. Perhaps potential new owners were puzzled by the garage, which Mr O'Carroll had designed himself. Faced with a steep drive leading up to the garage, Mr O'Carroll had built four steps to make access 'easier'. Just how he thought anyone could drive a car up four steps to get to the garage is not recorded. . .

Flipper Flop

A new MGM movie being shot in the summer of 1987 was called *A Fish Called Wanda.* The star of the film was a real flop who only lasted for one day's filming before being fired and ordered off the set. Her name? Wanda, a yellow angel fish. She lost the title role to another fish, a black and white one this time, who was presumably a better actress. . .

Gummed up

The British Postmaster General, Lord Lichfield, failed to spot a good idea when Rowland Hill went to him with his idea of a small piece of gummed paper that could be bought and applied to letters prior to postage. Lord Lichfield dismissed the idea, saying: 'Of all the wild, crackpot and idiotic schemes, this is the most foolish.' Despite him, postage stamps did appear for the first time in 1840.

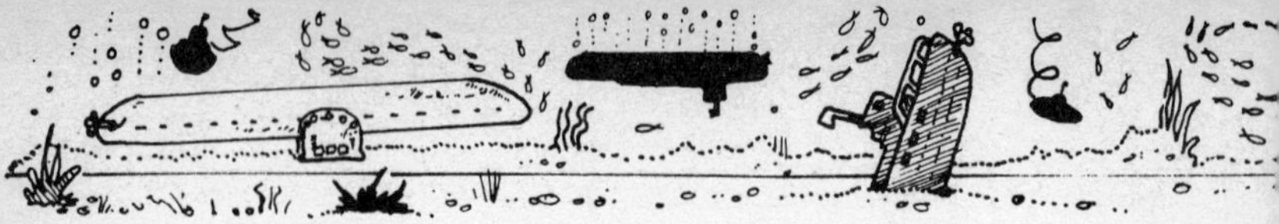

The Two-Car Town

Twin motoring flops have to be the two drivers who crashed head-on in the town of Redruth, in south-west England, in April 1906. Theirs were the only two cars in the town at that time. . .

Fame at Last

Frenchman, Clement Passal, wanted to sell his life story, but publishers didn't want to know. Clement imagined that he'd led an amazing life, but in truth he was just a small-time crook. Undeterred, he felt that he needed some headline-grabbing stunt to make people sit up and take notice of him, and, in 1929, he dreamed up a plan with an accomplice, Henri Boulogne. He wrote anonymous letters to newspapers, saying that he was part of a mysterious secret

society that had imprisoned Clement Passal. His plan was that he would make an amazing 'escape' and so find fame. But the idea flopped when the newspapers ignored the letters.

Clement then decided that he had to do something that could not fail to grab the attention of the newspapers. He wrote letters saying that the secret society which had captured Passal, had tortured him, and buried him alive. Clement carried a coffin to Versailles, near Paris, dug a deep hole, and climbed into the coffin. He attached a small air pipe to breathe through, and Boulogne covered the coffin with earth. Now Boulogne had to post the letters to the newspapers, and the journalists would follow the map and find the 'hero' Passal. He would be famous, and could sell his life story.

Unfortunately, Boulogne was very tired, and slept for many hours before posting the letters. That delay was tragic, for when police officers dug up the coffin, Clement Passal was dead. He was famous at last, but the plan had failed and cost him his life.

Canyon Fodder

Evel Knievel was a motorcycle stuntman who set lots of records for jumping his bike over long lines of cars and trucks. In 1974, he announced plans for a new jump – not vehicles this time, but the gaping Snake River Canyon in Idaho, USA! The canyon is some 400 metres (1300 feet) wide, and Evel planned to jump the distance on a rocket-powered motorcycle called the Sky-cycle.

The jump attracted a lot of media interest, and collected $21,000,000 from thousands of spectators and almost a million people watching closed-circuit television coverage across America. Spectators included actors Dustin Hoffman, John Wayne and Steve McQueen, and singer Elvis Presley who, like thousands of others, were keen to see 'the stunt of the century'.

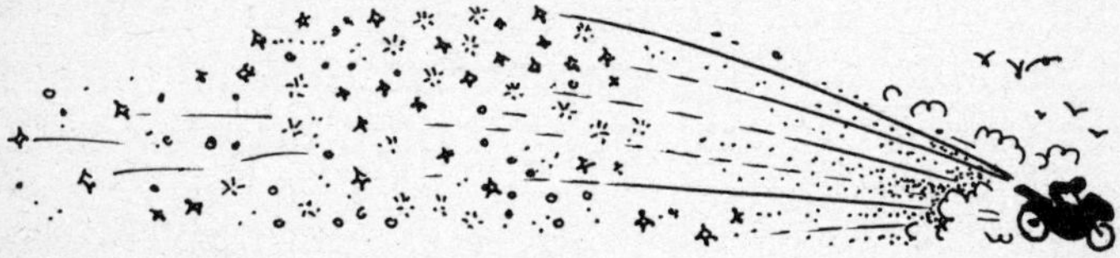

On 8 September, Evel's Sky-cycle took off with a roar from its rockets and gasps from the crowd. But instead of soaring across the canyon, the Sky-cycle dipped and plummeted 180 metres (600 feet) down into the gaping chasm. Safety parachutes fitted to the machine opened at once,

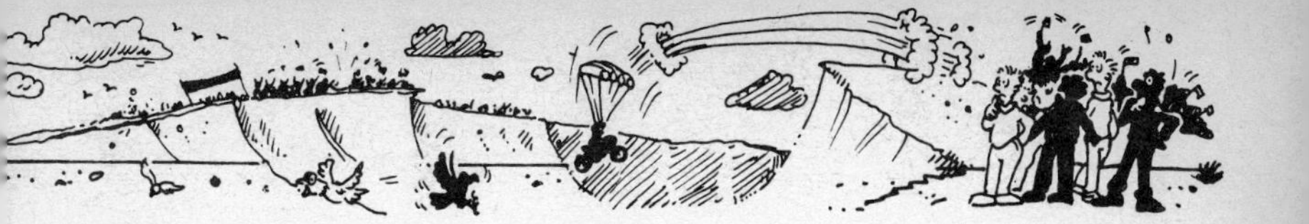

and it landed heavily at the bottom of the canyon. Luckily, Evel escaped with just a few cuts and bruises, but the Sky-cycle was wrecked. In a couple of seconds the stunt of the century had to be renamed the flop of the century.

Phew! What a Pong!

Sculptor Carl Andre was fed up with working in marble and stone, and decided to try something very different for his next exhibition. He designed what he thought was going to be the masterpiece of all time. What did he use – wire, cardboard, plastic? No – Carl's sculpture was made entirely of cheese blocks 25 centimetres (10 inches) thick – some 227 kilograms (500 pounds) in all! He stacked the cheese blocks artistically, then added the finishing touch by pouring 45 litres (10 gallons) of Tomato Ketchup over the top. The exhibition was a real flop that lasted one day because the hot lights made the cheese sculpture so smelly that no one got past the door to look at it. Carl decided to go back to stone. . .

Snailure

Marc Quinquandon of France was so fond of eating snails that he decided to set a world record for snail eating. He managed to eat 144 snails in a little over 11 minutes, and earned his place in the record books, but, not content with that, he decided to try for an even greater record. Marc ate 72 snails in just three minutes, but success turned to snailure . . . sorry, failure . . . when he died soon after. The cause of death? Snail poisoning.

Zzzzzzzzz. . .

Denis Santachiaria is an Italian furniture designer with lots of unusual ideas. One design that failed because it was so successful was a special sofa, unveiled in 1984. The sofa had a gentle swaying motion that was meant to relax the person sitting on it, but it worked so well that people went straight to sleep! After boring parties where all the guests fell asleep, the sofa was returned to its designer.

Fred's Moondial

Fred O'Brien is a graphic designer who lives and works in the north of England. In 1981, he sent detailed plans for a new idea to *Design Magazine*. His drawings and notes featured a new sundial design: a luminous pocket model with its own auxiliary light source, that could be used at night. Sundials show the time of day by shadows cast by the sun, and are no use at all at night, so the idea was an obvious joke.

Not so obvious. The magazine printed details of the design, and a television producer rang Mr O'Brien to ask if he could feature the idea. Mr O'Brien explained that the design was a joke. Next, an investor rang to ask if the sundial could be produced more cheaply in plastic? Mr O'Brien explained – again – that the moondial was a (failed) practical joke, but this didn't deter the investor, who soon had 150,000 portable night-use moondials made in Hong Kong. He just couldn't see the joke. . .

Back to the Drawing Board

Forgers of works of art have to do their research very carefully to make sure that every detail is correct. One who failed to do this was the man who produced a painting and said that it was the work of a 17th century French artist called Georges de la Tour. In 1960, the painting, called *The Fortune Teller,* was sold to the famous Metropolitan Museum of Art in New York, USA, for several million dollars. Art experts had said that the painting was a genuine de la Tour, but they failed to spot some odd features in it. The hairstyles of the figures in the paintings were much more 20th than 17th century, and one figure was dressed in a leather jacket that zipped at the front. Now zips weren't very common in 17th century France, in fact they weren't invented until 1891, so visitors to the museum started to smell a rat. The show was a flop, and the painting was removed from the museum's walls.

Impossible, I Say

Simon Newcomb was a famous American scientist and astronomer, born in 1835. He wrote many features and articles in newspapers and magazines saying that people could not fly in machines that were heavier than air. A few years later, in 1903, the Wright brothers, Wilbur and Orville, made their first short flights in just such heavier-than-air machines – the first planes. Despite this evidence, Newcomb still stuck to his belief that planes were an impossible dream. I wonder what he'd have said about people going to the moon?

Up, Up and. . . Now Way

Frank Fielder of Manchester, north-west England, likes to see his name in the newspapers, and has come up with various pranks to attract publicity. He planned a newsworthy trip in his hot-air balloon in 1986, but the idea flopped. He asked the Indian Prime Minister, Rajiv Gandhi, to fly with him – but had to cancel the trip when he found that his balloon basket wasn't big enough to carry Frank, the Prime Minister, and the 16 armed security guards who had to go everywhere with him!

Out for a Duck

Radio Telefis Eireann, the Irish National Broadcasting Service, heard about a record-breaking resident on a farm in Limerick, on the west coast of Ireland, and decided to feature him on a television news programme. Cameramen, sound recordists and an interviewer drove right across the country from Dublin to interview and film the celebrity – Ireland's oldest duck. Sadly, the news item was a real flop – the television crew's car ran over the duck as it turned into the farmyard. . .

A Cop Flop

Frank Thompson is an Australian with an unusual hobby – he collects ties and other unusual kinds of neckwear. In the summer of 1987 he asked if he could have an Australian Vice Squad police tie to add to his large collection, but his request was refused. Why? A spokesman for the Squad said that the tie could help Frank to imitate a police officer. But Frank would need a lot more than a tie to pass as a police officer as he's only 109 centimetres (43 inches) tall!

The Seasick Sailor

Lord Horatio Nelson was a great British naval hero who died after defeating the French and Spanish fleets at the battle of Trafalgar in 1805. Though a great leader, Nelson was a failure as a natural sailor – though he first went to sea at the age of 12, he suffered from very bad seasickness on every voyage.

Ear Ear

Mr Senby, who lived in Leeds, northern England, was deaf in one ear. He'd worn a hearing aid for 20 years, but didn't think much of it as it didn't seem to improve his hearing at all. The reason for the hearing aid's failure came to light when Mr Senby went for a hospital check up and the doctors there discovered that he'd been wearing the hearing aid in the wrong ear!

The (Non)Electric Chair

Emperor Menelik II ruled the African country of Abyssinia (now called Ethiopia) from 1844 to 1913. He was worried about the violence and murder in his country, and decided that a deterrent to criminals was called for. He read about the electric chair that had first been used in America for executing murderers, and decided that it was just what he needed. He ordered three electric chairs from an American manufacturer, and the chairs were sent by ship across the Atlantic, then by land to the country's capital Addis Ababa. Everyone congratulated Menelik on his great idea until workers unpacked the electric chairs and were forced to point out the fatal flaw in his plan – there was no electricity supply in Abyssinia at that time. . .

With no electricity to power them, the electric chairs were useless, but Menelik managed to save face by using one as his new throne!

A Batty Idea

American military scientists thought they'd come up with a great new idea when they planned to use bats as miniature 'flying bombs' by strapping incendiary devices to the animals and aiming them at enemy positions. The bats would fly to the target areas unnoticed, and the devices would be activated where they landed. The bats had other ideas, though, and tests flopped miserably when the animals ignored the trial targets they were aimed at, and flew on. They roosted for the night under the eaves of the roof of a nearby air base. The bombs went off, the air base burned down, and the flying bomb idea was quietly dropped.

False Economy

A bank note worth one cruzeiro was thought a good idea in Brazil – until it was discovered, in 1960, that it cost one and a half cruzeiros to print each note. . .

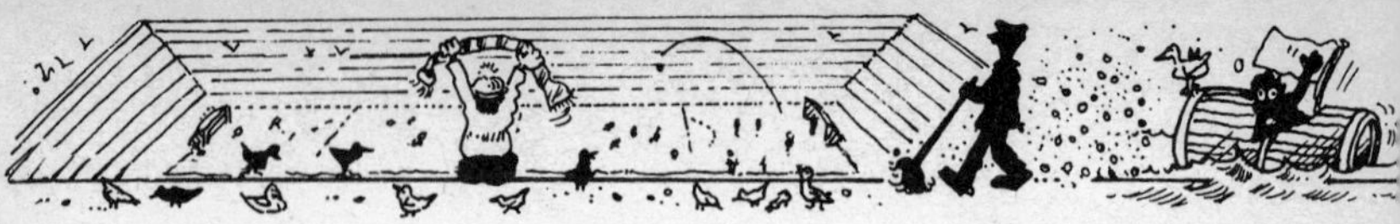

'I'm Strong to the Finish, Cause. . .

I eats my spinach,' says Popeye in the popular cartoon films. For many years, people believed that spinach had lots more iron than other vegetables, and that it made them extra-strong – just like Popeye. But a German scientist working in the 1930s discovered that the super-vegetable is really a flop, and has no more iron than other vegetables. The scientist who first measured the iron content of spinach had failed to notice that he'd put the decimal point in the wrong place, making spinach ten times richer in iron than it really was!

What Price Friendship?

Mike Molloy was a drunk who used to hang around in rough drinking houses in New York, USA, in the 1930s. Unknown to him, four so-called-friends of his came up with a money-making plan that could not fail. They planned to insure Mike's life for $1,500, kill him, then collect the cash. It sounded simple, but they didn't reckon on Mike's iron constitution. . .

The would-be murderers poisoned Mike's drink, but it didn't have much effect on him – he just became a little more drunk than usual. Plan two was carried out, but Mike enjoyed eating the poisoned oysters. Evidently, more drastic measures were needed, so the four men got Mike very drunk, then laid him in an alley and drove a car backwards and forwards over his body. Mike ended up in hospital, but made a full recovery, and was soon back. Mike's 'friends' then gave him sardine sandwiches that they had filled with shredded metal; he liked them, and asked for more! On a freezing winter night, the four men drugged Mike, stripped him of his clothes and doused him with cold water, then they left him outside in the snow all night. They hoped he'd catch pneumonia, but Mike didn't catch so much as a cold.

Finally, the four men drugged Mike one last time, and gassed him. They had succeeded in killing him at last, but their plan still failed, for they were convicted of his murder and were executed at Sing Sing Prison in June 1934.

The Cure That Killed

When King Charles II of England suffered a stroke in 1685, doctors were called to his bedside to come up with a cure. In all, 12 doctors treated the King. They decided to rid the King's body of all poisons, and took a litre (two pints) of his blood for starters. The doctors covered his body with hot plasters, ripped them off again (painful!) and filled his nose with snuff that made him sneeze uncontrollably.

As if that wasn't enough, the doctors then shaved the King's head and branded it with red-hot irons. Not surprisingly, these treatments all failed to help the King's condition. Undaunted, the doctors repeated all the procedures, and fed the King various 'cures' they had thought up, including powdered horse's skull, shredded rook feathers and bits of frogs. This treatment also failed, and the King died after five days – probably as a result of the 'cure'.

The Idea Just Snowballed

Arthur Pedrick is an ideas man from Selsey, in southern England, who calls himself the 'One Man Think Tank Basic Physics Research Laboratory'. He has patented many, many ideas over the years – none of which has been successful – including a golf ball that can be steered in flight and a car that can be driven from the back seat.

Perhaps his most ambitious plan was an idea he came up with to make the desert areas of the world suitable for agriculture. What was needed in the extremely dry conditions was, of course, water to irrigate the dry land. But how could it be arranged? Rainfall was almost non-existent, and a piped water supply was out of the question. Mr Pedrick soon came up with the answer, and on paper it sounds quite simple. A large number of giant pea-shooters would be built at the North and South Poles, and huge snowballs would be made from compacted snow. The snowballs would be loaded into the pea-shooters, which would be aimed at deserts, and fired by wind power. The desert areas would be hit by a constant stream of huge snowballs which would melt in the heat, and water the land so that crops could be grown. Not surprisingly, Mr Pedrick's plan was just one big wet flop. . .

Do, Re, Me, Fa, So, La, Te Aaarrgh!

In 1953, opera singer Walter Midgley was singing in *Rigoletto*, at the famous Opera House in Covent Garden, London, England. The audience was surprised when he failed to hit the high notes, and thought him rather a flop. But after the performance was over, Walter was able to explain his strange performance – he had swallowed his false moustache!

He Went Thataway. . .

Despite being a qualified pilot, American Douglas Corrigan's sense of direction was a flop, to say the least. Equipped with a map of the United States, plus a compass, Douglas flew out of a New York airport on 18 July, 1938. He planned to fly west across the country en route for Los Angeles, on the east coast. Sounds a simple journey, doesn't it? For a pilot with a normal sense of direction it would have been,

but Douglas wasn't heard of for the next 28 hours, and when he did touch down it wasn't in America, but in Dublin, capital of Ireland, on the other side of the Atlantic Ocean! He had flown in the wrong direction, and put his mistake down to a miscalculation when he set his compass. The first trans-Atlantic flight had been made only 11 years before, and Douglas had to admit that he was 'pretty tired' after his epic journey. Not surprisingly, the newspaper gave the failed navigator a new nickname: 'Wrong Way Corrigan'.

Gotcha!

Piers Gayle dressed in his best clothes before trying to rob a supermarket in Sweden. His plan to charm the check-out girl into handing over money failed miserably, though, when he leaned towards the open cash drawer of the till and the girl slammed it shut, trapping his tie. Piers was still trapped in the till when the police arrived.

Tell It to the (Sub)Marines

In 1624, a Dutchman called Cornelius von Drebel went to the British Admiralty with some amazing drawings of a new craft which he thought might be useful to them. The Admiralty looked at his plans, and dismissed his idea as a silly novelty that would never work. Von Drebel had designed the first submarine. . .

A Communications Breakdown

A newspaper reporter failed badly when he tried to file his story to *The Times* by telephone. He dictated a long and learned article on the Dead Sea Scrolls, important ancient documents found in Palestine in 1947. When the paper was published he was horrified to find it under the headline: 'Dead Sea Squirrels'!

Money, Money, Money

WC Fields, the famous American comic and actor, joked about anything and everything – except money. To him, money was a serious matter, to be earned, banked, but not to be spent unless absolutely necessary. He was so afraid of losing even small amounts of money that, as soon as he had a pocketful of loose change, he would bank it, rather than risk even a single small coin dropping from his pocket unnoticed. Fields travelled across America almost continuously, but this didn't deter him; he opened new bank accounts wherever he happened to be, in Dallas or Denver, Baltimore or Buffalo. He never used his own name, but dreamed up aliases like Figley Whitesides or Ludovic Fishpond. Soon he had hundreds of small accounts all over America. But Fields' miserly plan was a flop in the end, because he opened so many accounts, in so many different places, using so many different names that he forgot about most of them. More than 40 years after his death, there are still hundreds of bank accounts across the length and breadth of America just waiting to be claimed. Fields must be turning in his grave at the thought of all that unclaimed cash. . .

There's No Smoke Without Chimneys

Builders of the new Howard Hotel in Baltimore, USA, lit fires in the rooms to air the huge building – and then found that they'd failed to build any chimneys. . .

Four-legged Works of Art

In the 1920s, in New York State, USA, deer-hunting was very popular. So popular, in fact, that at weekends the countryside was crawling with hunters who hardly knew one end of a gun from the other. They shot at anything that moved – sometimes they even shot at each other, though they usually missed!

By 1927, farmers were so fed up of having their milk cows shot at in mistake for deer that they came up with an idea. They painted their cows in shades of khaki, green and brown so that they blended into the countryside and could graze undisturbed. This didn't work very well as the hunters still spotted movement – and shot at the cows. The next year the farmers painted their cows again, but this time they used bright, vivid colours, and painted their cows in stripes, spots and other bright patterns so that the hunters just couldn't mistake them for deer. After all, whoever saw a pink deer with blue polka dots?

The hunters certainly saw the cows now, but the painted cows idea failed in the end – the normally docile cows didn't like the bright colours and patterns, and became upset and hard to handle. When they stopped giving milk the farmers had to wash the paint off, and go back to the drawing board.

The end of the World is Nigh

Jehovah's Witnesses flopped in the business of making predictions about the future when they said that the world would end in 1984. It didn't. . .

Horse Laugh

At the Royal Windsor Horse Show held in southern England in 1982, a competition was held. First prize was a signed portrait of the famous racehorse, Red Rum. The organizers couldn't understand why no one bothered to enter the competition until someone admitted that they thought it was a joke. 'We all know Red Rum is a great horse', he explained, 'but no one has ever claimed that he can sign his own name!'

Fly Me To . . . Detroit

The biggest flop as a plane hijacker was the man who boarded a plane in New York in 1976 and demanded that the crew fly him to Detroit. He needn't have bothered – the plane was bound for Detroit anyway . . .